NEW STEPS IN

RELIGIOUS EDUCATION

Book 2

NEW EDITION

Michael Keene

First published in 1991.
Second edition 1997 by:
Stanley Thornes (Publishers) Ltd

Reprinted in 2001 by:
Nelson Thornes Ltd
Delta Place
27 Bath Road
CHELTENHAM
GL53 7TH
United Kingdom

01 02 03 04 05 / 10 9 8

A catalogue record for this book is available from the British Library

First edition ISBN 0 871402 38 7
Second edition ISBN 0 7487 3078 8

Illustrations by Gillian Hunt and Peters & Zabransky
Second edition page make-up by Penny Mills
Picture research by Christina Morgan
Edited by Victoria Ramsay

Printed and bound in China by Midas

Acknowledgements

With thanks to the following for permission to reproduce photographs and other material in this book:

AKG Photos p.36 ● Ancient Art & Architecture Collection p.30 ● Andes Press Agency pp.66, 67, 88
● Chris Fairclough Colour Library pp.13, 19, 95 ● Robert Harding Picture Library p.84 ● Michael Holford
pp.15, 26 ● Hutchison Library pp.31, 92, 93 ● Magnum p.89 ● Christine Osborne pp.68, 82
● Ann and Bury Peerless p.27 ● Peter Sanders Photography pp.85, 91 ● Peter Trainer p.18 ● The Walking
Camera pp.4, 5, 7, 8, 9, 16, 17, 20, 21, 22, 24, 25, 28, 29, 32, 33, 34, 35, 38, 39, 40, 41, 43, 44, 45, 46, 47,
48, 49, 50, 51, 52, 53, 54, 55, 56, 57, 58, 59, 62, 63, 64, 65, 71, 72, 73, 74, 75, 76, 77, 78, 79, 80, 94.

Every effort has been made to contact copyright holders and we apologise if any have been inadvertently
overlooked.

The scripture quotations are taken from the Holy Bible, New International Version ®. Copyright © 1973,
1978, 1984 by International Bible Society. Used by permission of International Bible Society. 'NIV' and
'New International Version' are trademarks registered in the United States Patent and Trademark office by
International Bible Society.

Throughout the series the terms BCE (Before Common Era) and CE (Common Era) are used instead of the
more familiar BC and AD. However, in practice, they mean the same thing.

Contents

1

How did it all begin?

Jesus was a Jew. He lived about two thousand years ago in the tiny land of Palestine, a country in the Middle East which is now called Israel. Palestine was about the same size as Wales. For a long time it was under Roman control and when Jesus was born it was ruled over by **Herod the Great**, who was a Jew. The Romans had put Herod on the throne and he did exactly as he was told. He was there to keep the Jews under control and he did this very effectively. He was a very cruel king.

Jesus

The Jews hated being under Roman control and many of them asked God to send them a leader who would free them. This leader was known as the **Messiah** and many people believed that Jesus was the one for whom they had been waiting. They were disappointed. Jesus was neither a warrior nor an earthly king who could overthrow the Romans. He grew up in an ordinary Jewish family and tried to show the people how to live by his teaching and example.

For three years Jesus travelled around Palestine with his twelve **disciples** or followers (see picture A) who were chosen by him to continue his work after he had left the earth. The **Gospels** show that Jesus spent much of his time teaching the people about God through **parables** or stories, arguing with the Jewish religious leaders, caring for the poor and sick, and performing miracles.

Jesus built up a large following among the people and this disturbed the religious authorities. They thought that he was becoming too powerful with the people. They wanted Jesus dead. Eventually **Pontius Pilate**, the Roman governor, signed a death warrant (see picture B). Pilate accepted that Jesus represented a threat to the Roman Empire. The Romans crucified him (killed him on a cross) on a hill just outside the city of **Jerusalem** in 29 CE.

The Resurrection

Three days after his crucifixion, the Gospels tell us that Jesus rose from the dead. This event, known as the **Resurrection**, is the most important Christian belief. Forty days later Jesus left the earth altogether. Before doing so, however, he told his followers that they must

A

What do you think Jesus was looking for when he chose twelve friends to travel with him?

B

...tations of the Cross are pictures or carvings which tell the story of Jesus on the way to his crucifixion. Why is Jesus seen here before Pontius Pilate?

preach his message throughout the world. They were so successful in doing this that by the fourth century the Roman Empire was ruled by a Christian emperor.

Words to remember

Disciple One of the twelve companions chosen by Jesus. After his death and Resurrection they were called 'apostles', which means 'those who have been sent'.

Gospels The word means 'good news' and is the name for the four books in the Bible which give an account of Jesus's life and teaching.

Herod the Great (70–4 BCE) A king who ruled over Palestine with great brutality and rebuilt the Jewish Temple in Jerusalem.

Jerusalem The capital city of Palestine. It is the home of the Temple where the Jews worshipped until it was destroyed by the Romans in 70 CE.

Messiah God's leader who, the Jews believed, would deliver them from Roman domination.

Parable A story told by Jesus to teach people a religious or moral lesson.

Pontius Pilate The Roman governor of Judea from 26–36 CE. Later he fell into disgrace and committed suicide.

Resurrection The most important Christian belief, that Jesus rose from the dead three days after being crucified and buried.

Do you know

◇ in which country Jesus lived and who controlled it at the time?
◇ which special leader the Jews were waiting for when Jesus was born?
◇ what happened at the end of the life of Jesus on earth?

Things to do

1 Write a sentence to answer each of these questions:
a Why did Jesus disappoint many Jews during his lifetime?
b Why did Jesus choose twelve disciples?
c What did Jesus spend most of his time on earth doing?
d What do Christians believe happened after Jesus was put to death?

2 In this extract from one of his letters, St Paul, one of the greatest leaders of the early Church, described to some young Christians in the town of Philippi what Jesus did:

> 'Who, being in very nature God... made himself nothing, taking the very nature of a servant, being made in human likeness. And being found in appearance as a man, he humbled himself and became obedient to death – even death on a cross!'

(Philippians 2.6–8)

Use this text to help you to answer these questions:
a What do you think it means to say that Jesus appeared on earth in 'human likeness'?
b St Paul says that Jesus 'became obedient to death'. What do you think he meant by this?
c Write your own summary of the life, death and Resurrection of Jesus. Try not to write more than 50 words.

What happened on the Day of Pentecost?

The Day of Pentecost is described in the **Acts of the Apostles**, the book in the Bible which comes after the Gospels in the **New Testament**. It is an account of the beginning and the early years of the Christian Church. It was written in about 75 CE by **Luke**, who also wrote the Gospel which carries his name.

The Day of Pentecost

After Jesus left the earth his disciples huddled together in a room in Jerusalem. They felt very alone and didn't know how they were going to carry on Jesus's work. They were also frightened that the Romans would arrest them as well. It didn't happen. Instead, God's **Holy Spirit** came over them and each of them began to speak in different languages. Luke's description of this event is in the information box.

The reason for the disciples speaking in strange languages soon becomes clear. At this time people from many different countries had gathered in Jerusalem for the very important Jewish festival of **Pentecost**. The disciples were now able to preach to them in their own language. You can see from the map below where these people had come from.

When the festival finished they returned home. Many believed the message they had heard and became Christian disciples. Through them the message began to spread well beyond the city of Jerusalem and into the Roman Empire.

Understanding the events

Christians do not agree amongst themselves as to exactly what happened on the Day of Pentecost. There are those who think that the event took place just as Luke describes it in the Acts of the Apostles. Others insist that Luke was using symbols (fire and wind) to try to put over some of the excitement and bewilderment of the experience (see picture B). All Christians would agree, however, that this was the birth of the Christian Church. From this moment onwards, the very disciples who had been terrified by recent events went out fearlessly to preach the Christian message.

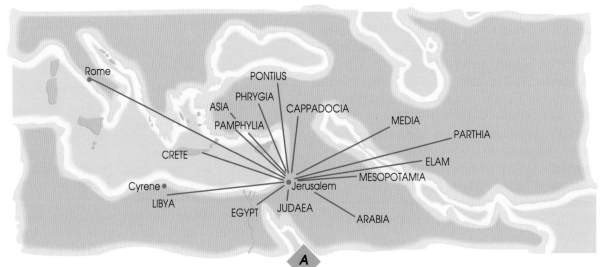

A

Why were so many people in Jerusalem at this time and what impact did the events of the Day of Pentecost have on many of them?

Words to remember

Acts of the Apostles The fifth book in the New Testament which tells the story of the Christian Church from the ascension of Christ into heaven to the imprisonment of Paul in Rome.

Holy Spirit The third person in the Christian Trinity active as God's presence in the world.

Luke The author of one of the Gospels and the Acts of the Apostles. He accompanied Paul on some of his missionary journeys.

New Testament The second part of the Bible that tells the Christian story and also contains letters written by church leaders.

Pentecost A Jewish festival which commemorates the giving of the Torah (Jewish law) to Moses. On this day, Christians remember when the Holy Spirit came to Jesus's disciples.

B

Why is fire associated with the coming of the Holy Spirit on the Day of Pentecost?

The Day of Pentecost

'When the Day of Pentecost came, they were all together in one place. Suddenly a sound like the blowing of a violent wind came from heaven and filled the whole house where they were sitting. They saw what seemed to be tongues of fire that separated and came to rest on each of them. All of them were filled with the Holy Spirit and began to speak in other tongues as the Spirit enabled them.

Now there were staying in Jerusalem God-fearing Jews from every nation under heaven. When they heard this sound, a crowd came together in bewilderment, because each one heard them speaking in his own language.'

(Acts 2.1–6)

Does this strike you as an account of something that actually took place, or a symbolic description of an event?

Do you know

◇ the state of the disciples when the events of the Day of Pentecost took place?
◇ why the gift of speaking in other languages appears to have been given to the early disciples?
◇ why this event is so important in the history of the Christian Church?

Things to do

1 Throughout the Church's history the Holy Spirit has often been pictured as a dove. Find out why by reading Luke 3.21–2. In your own words, describe this reason in your book.

2 Copy the map opposite into your book. Find out the modern names for three of the countries shown.

3 Imagine that you are an early Christian disciple who has been shattered and disillusioned by the death of Jesus. Describe the impact that the Resurrection of Jesus followed by the coming of the Holy Spirit on the Day of Pentecost has had upon you.

Who were Peter and Paul?

In the early Christian Church two people, **Peter** and **Paul**, were singled out as its first great leaders.

Peter

Peter was born in the small fishing port of Bethsaida, on the shores of Lake Galilee. His fisherman father called him Simon but Jesus re-named him 'Peter' from the Greek word meaning 'a rock'. Jesus said that Peter was the 'rock' on which he would build the Christian Church.

No disciple of Jesus plays as large a part in the Gospels as Peter. We have a picture of him as a hasty and hot-blooded man who often opened his mouth without thinking first. In spite of this, though, he seemed to understand things about Jesus that the other disciples failed to grasp. He was, for instance, the first disciple to see that Jesus was God's Messiah. After the Resurrection, he was one of the first to meet the risen Jesus and he became the first recognised leader of the early Church.

Some people believe that Peter became the first Bishop of Rome. We know the Bishop of Rome better as the **Pope**, the leader of the **Roman Catholic Church**. This would mean that the Pope is the successor of St Peter. Other Christian Churches do not accept this. We do know that Peter was crucified by the Emperor Nero in 64 CE, probably upside down as he did not want to die in the same way as Jesus.

Paul

Paul was a Roman citizen and originally a **Pharisee** – that is, a member of a strict religious Jewish group. They strongly opposed Jesus, seeing him as a threat to their beliefs. At first Paul persecuted the Christians, but on the way to Damascus he underwent a dramatic **conversion** and became one of the disciples. After he became a Christian, Paul dedicated the rest of his life to travelling throughout the Roman Empire preaching about Jesus. During these travels his life was very eventful:

◆ He was put into prison and flogged.
◆ He was seized by a mob and almost lynched before Roman soldiers saved him.
◆ He was shipwrecked on his way to Rome to stand trial.

Paul was greatly respected and wrote many letters both to churches and to individual Christians and some of these are written down in the New Testament. They are the oldest Christian documents to have survived. We are not sure how Paul died but it is likely that he was beheaded around the time that Peter was crucified.

CATHOLIC CHURCH
OF
SS. PETER AND PAUL
COMBE DOWN
A.D. 1965

MASS:	Saturday 6·00 p.m.	Sunday 9·30 a.m.
	Eve of Holyday	7·00 p.m.
	Holyday	11·00 a.m.
	Weekday	9·30 a.m.
RECONCILIATION:	Saturday	10·00 a.m. & 5·00 p.m.

A
This church has been named after Saints Peter and Paul. What do you think that members of this church might find in the lives of these great men to inspire them?

Do you know

◇ what Peter's first name was and why it was changed by Jesus?
◇ who is thought by many Christians to be the modern successor of Peter?
◇ how Paul became a Christian?

Words to remember

Conversion   A dramatic and unexpected turnaround in beliefs.

Paul   A strict religious Jew who was very much against the Church. After a dramatic conversion he became one of its most important leaders and worked tirelessly to spread the Christian message.

Peter   The disciple that Jesus singled out to be the leader of the early Church.

Pharisee   A member of a strongly religious Jewish group that frequently came into conflict with Jesus.

Pope   The head of the Roman Catholic Church who lives in the Vatican in Rome. He is also called the Bishop of Rome.

Roman Catholic Church   The largest of all the different Christian Churches.

Things to do

the Damascus Road. (His name was Saul before he became a Christian.)

'As he neared Damascus on his journey suddenly a light from heaven flashed around him. He fell to the ground and heard a voice say to him, "Saul, Saul, why do you persecute me?"

"Who are you, Lord?" Saul asked.

"I am Jesus, whom you are persecuting," he replied. "Now get up and go into the city, and you will be told what you must do."

The men travelling with Saul stood there speechless; they heard the sound but did not see anyone. Saul got up from the ground, but when he opened his eyes he could see nothing. So they led him by the hand into Damascus. For three days he was blind, and did not eat or drink anything.'

(Acts 9.3–9)

Divide the class into groups of about six. Imagine that one member of each group is a local radio reporter sent to cover this dramatic event. Make a tape recording describing the scene soon after the event. Carry out interviews with the people who were travelling with Paul – and with the great man himself. Try to find out as much as you can about what happened, and how it affected those who were there. Make sure that everyone in the group has a part to play.

1 This stained-glass window shows Peter holding the keys to the Kingdom of Heaven. You can read the background to this in Matthew 16.13–20, which you should look at carefully before answering these questions:

a Who did the people think that Jesus was?

b Who did Peter recognise Jesus to be?

c Who did Jesus say had revealed the truth to Peter?

d What did Jesus promise Peter?

2 Look at Luke's description in the Acts of the Apostles of the conversion of Paul on

How did the Roman Empire become Christian?

Peter and Paul were not the only missionaries in the early Church. Apart from known disciples such as Thomas, who is believed to have preached in India, hundreds of unknown believers talked about their faith wherever they went. You can see how rapidly the Christian faith spread by looking at the map below.

Persecution

From time to time the early Christians were **persecuted**. Some of the Roman emperors tried to wipe out the Christian religion, believing it to be a threat to the empire. **Nero** was one such ruler. In 64 CE he blamed the Christians for a fire in Rome which he himself had started. He rounded up hundreds of Christians and slaughtered them. No one knows just how many died at his hands. Nor do we know how many were put to death by other emperors. We do know, though, that many were thrown to the lions in the Colosseum in Rome.

Constantine's conversion

At the start of the fourth century everything changed. **Constantine** was involved in a bitter battle with a rival, Maxentius, over who should become emperor. Constantine prayed to the 'Supreme God' to help him. The response was a sign – a cross in the noon-day sky above the sun with the words 'Conquer by this'. That night, Constantine claimed, Christ appeared to him in a dream and told him to use the sign of the cross at the head of his army whenever it went into battle.

Constantine obeyed, miraculously his armies won and the new emperor ensured that the Christian religion was officially recognised throughout the Roman Empire. The days of persecution for the Christians at the hands of the Romans were over. Yet the victory was short-lived. The Roman Empire was already showing signs of crumbling. In less than a century its armies had withdrawn from most parts of the empire before it disappeared altogether.

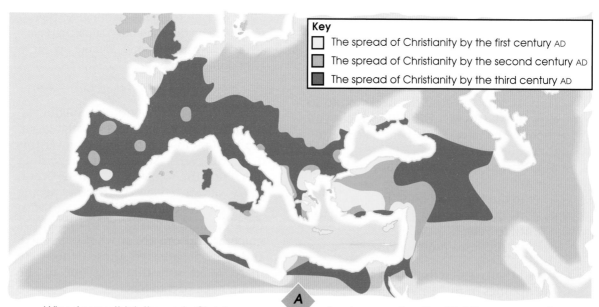

Key
- ☐ The spread of Christianity by the first century AD
- ☐ The spread of Christianity by the second century AD
- ☐ The spread of Christianity by the third century AD

A
Why do you think the early Christians were so effective in spreading the Christian message?

Tacitus speaks

Tacitus was a Roman historian who lived through the reign of Nero. He tells how the emperor treated the Christians:

'First those who confessed to being Christians were arrested. Then, on information obtained from them, hundreds were convicted, more for their anti-social beliefs than for fire-raising. In their deaths they were made a mockery. They were covered in the skins of wild animals, torn to death by dogs, crucified or set on fire – so that when darkness fell they burned like torches in the night. Nero opened up his own gardens for this spectacle and gave a show in the arena, where he mixed with the crowd, or stood dressed as a charioteer on a chariot.'

Explain, in your own words, what kind of person you think Nero was.

Words to remember

Constantine   He came to power in 312 CE and was the first emperor to accept Christianity.

Nero   Roman emperor from 54–68 CE, Nero acted with great cruelty towards the Christian Church and anyone else who opposed him.

Persecute   To hunt down and torture or put someone to death for their religious beliefs.

Do you know

◇ why some Roman emperors tried to wipe out the Christian faith?
◇ who blamed the Christians for a fire that he himself started in Rome, and what revenge he took on them?
◇ who the first Christian Roman emperor was and what difference it made to the Christian Church?

Do you think that it is likely that Jesus really appeared to Constantine? If not, how do you think this story might have arisen in the first place? **B**

Things to do

1 Imagine that you are a Christian in the reign of Nero. He has been rounding up your Christian friends and cruelly putting them to death. Keep a diary recording your thoughts and actions as you expect the Roman soldiers to arrive and arrest you at any time.

2 Tertullian was a Christian writer who lived through much of the Roman persecution. In this extract he tries to explain why the early Christians were singled out for such harsh treatment:

'If the river Tiber reaches the walls, if the river Nile does not rise to the fields, if the sky does not move or the earth does, if there is a famine, if there is a plague, the cry is at once "The Christians to the lions". What, all of them to one lion?'

a Why do you think that each of the natural disasters mentioned here was blamed on the early Christians?
b Look in a dictionary to discover what a 'scapegoat' is. Do you think that this word accurately describes the position of Christians in the Roman Empire?

How did Christianity arrive in Britain?

No one is quite sure how, or when, the Christian message first arrived in Britain. Probably some of the Roman soldiers sent to Britain were Christians. The spread of Christianity in those early days is usually associated with the work of a handful of people.

St Ninian

St Ninian has been described as the 'first and the greatest of the ancient Christian missionaries' yet we know almost nothing about him. It is certain, however, that he worked amongst the Picts in east Scotland and built a **monastery** at Whitehorn.

St Patrick

More is known about **St Patrick** (389–461 CE). At the age of sixteen he was kidnapped from his father's farm in the west of Britain and taken to Ireland. During his six years of slavery there, his faith in God grew. Until then religion had meant little to him but, as a captive of heathen masters who had no faith in God, his own prayers became very important:

> 'Day by day as I went, a shepherd with my flock, I used to pray constantly... a hundred prayers a day, and nearly as many at night, staying out in the woods or on a mountain. And before daybreak I was up for prayer, in snow or frost or rain.'

One night a voice told Patrick in a dream, 'Your ship is ready'. He managed to escape from slavery and walk 200 miles to the nearest port. He arrived back in England only to hear in his mind the people of Ireland begging him:

> 'We beseech [beg] you to come and walk among us once more.'

In 432 CE Patrick returned to spend the last 30 years of his life in Ireland. Although not well educated himself, he encouraged learning and the building of many monasteries. Many

What does Patrick appear to be doing in this picture?

miracles were connected with him, as you can see from picture A above. Here he is banishing frogs and other vermin into the marshes.

St Columba

Ireland was the birthplace of **St Columba** (521–597 CE) who became a famous **abbot** and missionary. In 563 CE, along with twelve friends, he set out from Irish shores to undertake a '**pilgrimage** for Christ'. The pilgrimage took them to **Iona** on the western coast of Scotland. Here Columba established a monastery and started to preach to people who knew nothing about the Christian faith. Iona was to remain Columba's headquarters for thirty-four years whilst he and his followers converted a large part of Scotland to Christianity. Iona is now one of the most important destinations for pilgrims in Britain.

Do you know ?

◇ how the Christian religion probably first arrived in Britain?
◇ why St Patrick returned to Ireland as a missionary?
◇ which famous religious community was founded by St Columba?

B

Thousands of Christians go to Iona each year for prayer and relaxation. Why do you think it is still a special place for so many people?

Words to remember

Abbot The head of a monastery.

Iona A small island in the Inner Hebrides off the west coast of Scotland where St Columba founded a monastery in 563 CE.

Monastery The building in which monks live and worship.

Pilgrimage A journey taken for a religious reason to a holy place.

St Columba A famous abbot and missionary, who established the religious community at Iona.

St Ninian A very early Christian missionary, who built a monastery and worked in east Scotland.

St Patrick He took the Christian message to Ireland.

Things to do

1 Most of our information about St Columba comes from *The Life of St Columba* written by Adamnan, Abbot of Iona from 679–704 CE. Here are some extracts:

'From boyhood he had given himself as a Christian recruit to studies in quest of wisdom... God bestowed on him a sound body and a pure mind... he was angelic in appearance, bright in speech, holy in deeds, excellent in gifts and great in counsel. He could not let an hour go past without applying himself to prayer, reading, writing or some sort of work... he was dear to everybody, always showing a cheerful, holy face.'

a Explain what you think each of these phrases means:
   ◆ 'a sound body and a pure mind'
   ◆ 'he was angelic in appearance, bright in speech, holy in deeds, excellent in gifts and great in counsel'.
b Imagine that Columba has just died. Using the information you are given here, write an obituary for a newspaper. (An obituary is a summary of someone's life, character and achievements.)

2 An Irish legend describes how a witch threw garlic water at St Patrick as part of a spell to kill him. The saint, however, promptly threw back a hand-ball and this killed the witch on the spot. After the angels had comforted him, Patrick is believed to have prayed that Ireland would never lose its Christian faith.
a Why do you think that stories about miracles like this grew up in the first place?
b Try to find out other legends about saints. Tell each other your stories. Choose the most interesting ones and divide into groups. Each group should then write up one story and draw pictures to illustrate it. Put all the stories and illustrations together to make a wall display.

Why was St Augustine important?

In the sixth century a **monk** in Rome named **Gregory** saw some blond-haired children, playing in the market-place. They looked quite different from the Romans. On asking about them, he discovered that they were 'Anglii' (Latin, meaning 'from England'), the children of English slaves, and that they were heathen (having no Christian belief). His famous reply was that the children were 'Angels and not Anglii'.

The arrival of Augustine in England

When he became Pope, Gregory did not forget what he had seen. In 596 CE he sent a team of forty monks under **Augustine** to England. When they landed, Augustine sent a message to King Ethelbert telling him that they had come from Rome

> 'bringing good news of everlasting joy in heaven and a Kingdom that knows no end, with the true and living God.'

After much thought, the king told them they could stay and within a few months he had followed his queen in becoming a Christian (see picture A). He gave the monks a palace in **Canterbury** and allowed them to preach freely. Today Canterbury Cathedral (picture B) is the centre of the **Anglican** faith throughout the world.

A What do you think Augustine is saying to King Ethelbert and Queen Bertha? What might their reply have been?

The two groups

Pope Gregory sent a message to Augustine advising him that the English should be brought round slowly from belief in their old gods to the Christian faith. There were, in fact, already many Christians in Britain but they did not readily accept the preaching of Augustine. For almost a century these two groups had little to do with each other. There is no denying, though, Augustine's success as a large number of English people became Christians as a result of his missionary work.

A hermit's advice

Much of our information about this period comes from the Venerable Bede, a scholar and writer. Augustine organised a conference for British bishops and Bede tells us of the advice they were given by a hermit (a monk who lives alone):

> 'If he [Augustine] is a man of God, follow him. How shall we know? Our Lord said "I am meek and lowly of heart". If he is meek and lowly he may bear the yoke of Christ. But how shall we know? Let him arrive first. When you come in, if he rise up and greet you, hear him submissively [listen to him]. If not, he despises you and I say, despise you him.'

◇ There is one part of this advice which is surprising coming, as it does, from one Christian to other Christians. What do you think it is?
◇ Why is it surprising?

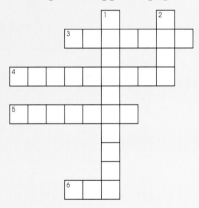

B
This cathedral at Canterbury is built on the site given to Augustine by King Ethelbert. Why do you think this place is particularly important to Anglicans throughout the world?

Do you know

◇ why Pope Gregory sent Augustine to England?
◇ where Augustine set up his headquarters?
◇ what reception Augustine received from those who were already Christians and what success his mission had?

Words to remember

Anglican   A worldwide fellowship of different Churches, based upon the teachings of the Church of England.

Augustine   A monk sent by Pope Gregory to be a missionary in England; he became the first Archbishop of Canterbury in 597 CE.

Canterbury   The place in Kent in the south of England where Augustine set up his headquarters. The Archbishop of Canterbury is the leader of the Anglican Church throughout the world.

Gregory   A Roman monk who built many monasteries and was elected Pope in 590 CE.

Monk   A male member of a religious community.

Things to do

1 Copy out and fill in the following crossword. How many can you do without looking at the opposite page?

1 The headquarters of Augustine (10)
2 This monk was a famous writer (4)
3 Having no Christian beliefs (7)
4 Leader of the team of monks sent to Britain by Pope Gregory (9)
5 This Pope advised bringing the English round slowly to the Christian faith (7)
6 Augustine told King Ethelbert that he would find this in heaven (3)

2 The Venerable Bede wrote this about the success of Augustine's mission:

'Then greater numbers began to come together to hear the word and to forsake their heathen ways and join the church. The King was known to be pleased at their faith and conversion, not that he would drive anyone to the Christian fold, for those who prepared him for baptism had taught him that one must choose to serve Christ, not be forced to it.'

a Why were those who joined the church expected to change their 'heathen ways'?
b Why did King Ethelbert not force his subjects to become Christians?

Why are there so many different Churches?

The Christian Church today is divided into many different Churches or **denominations**. There are now thought to be over 20,000 worldwide and new ones are starting up all the time. To find out why the Christian Church first began to split up in this way we must look back into history.

The start of Christianity

Within a few years of the death of Jesus, Christianity had spread through most of the Roman Empire and within three centuries it had become its official religion. As the Christian message extended to other parts of the world, the Church began to split up into many of the denominations that we have today with similar Christian beliefs but different ways of worship.

Branches of the one Church

It is very important to remember that the various denominations are different 'branches' of the Christian Church and not different religions. Most of the branches which exist today fall into one of four groups:

◆ The Roman Catholic Church. This is the oldest Christian Church, with 1,000 million followers worldwide. Its headquarters are in the Vatican City – a small, self-governing state in Rome. The head of the Catholic Church is the Pope, whom followers believe to be the successor of St Peter (see page 8). About 60 per cent of all Christians belong to the Roman Catholic Church.

◆ The **Orthodox Church**. This family of Churches came into existence after a split with the Roman Catholic Church in 1054. Although this Church was originally based in Constantinople, most Orthodox Christians are now found in Russia and Greece.

◆ The **Protestant Church**. During the sixteenth century the Reformation took place in Europe. This was a movement to return to the basic Christian principles. It was a protest against the Catholic Church which was corrupt at the time. At this time in England, King Henry VIII quarrelled with the Pope because he would not allow the king to divorce. As a result, the King set himself up as head of the Church in England. It was not until the reign of

A
This photograph shows an Orthodox church. Write down five things that you notice about it.

Elizabeth I, that all their ties with the Roman Catholic Church were broken. The Church of England became the official (Established) Church.

◆ The **Nonconformist Churches**. These are Protestant groups which became separated from the Church of England from the seventeenth century onwards. Amongst the Noncomformist Churches are the Baptists, the Methodists and the Salvation Army.

The Ecumenical Movement

Since 1945, many Christians from different denominations have increasingly worked together. Although there are few signs that the various Churches actually want to unite, they now talk and pray together regularly. Some of them celebrate **Holy Communion** together as a sign of their spiritual unity but this still does not happen between the larger Churches. This coming together is known as the **Ecumenical Movement**.

Do you know

◇ what a Christian 'denomination' is?
◇ why the Christian Church has split up into many different Christian denominations?
◇ what the main Christian denominations are?

Words to remember

Church of England The official Church in England, which recognises the king or queen as its head. It is one of the Protestant Churches.

Denomination A group of Churches with the same basic Christian beliefs but various styles of worship.

Ecumenical Movement An attempt in the second half of the twentieth century to bring together the main Christian denominations.

Holy Communion The most important service for most Christian denominations. It celebrates the last meal Jesus took with his disciples before his death.

Nonconformist Churches These are Protestant groups that do not belong to the Anglican, Orthodox or Roman Catholic denominations.

Orthodox Church This is a family of Churches made up of Russian and Greek Orthodox Christians together with members of other, smaller Churches.

Protestant Church Formed in the sixteenth century as a protest against corruption in the Roman Catholic Church, this is made up of the Church of England and other smaller denominations.

Things to do

1 In your book, answer each of these questions in complete sentences:
  a How long did it take Christianity to become the official religion of the Roman Empire?
  b Which denomination has about 60 per cent of all Christians in its membership?
  c Which Church has most of its members in Russia and Greece?

2 There are many different places of Christian worship. Try to find out how many different churches there are in your area. You might like to find out a little

more about one that specially interests you.

What about the Christian Church today?

Since the earliest days of the Christian Church, missionaries have been important in spreading the Christian message. Paul travelled far and wide, teaching about Jesus, and in the sixth century Augustine and his fellow monks made many converts to Christianity in England. Much later, in 1792, William Carey, a Northampton-shire cobbler, trod in their footsteps when he left England to be a missionary in India. He was the first 'modern' missionary.

The London City Mission

Since Carey countless other people have gone to work overseas combining teaching about Christianity with looking after those in need. Others have stayed at home. The London City Mission, for example, was set up in 1835 to help the poor and needy in Britain's capital city. Today the LCM has 130 full-time and voluntary

A

How do you think a London City Missioner might help this person?

missioners active in London's markets, housing estates, shops, factories and theatres (see picture A). There are now similar missions in other large cities in Britain such as Birmingham, Manchester and Glasgow.

The Salvation Army

The work of the **Salvation Army** started in 1880. The Army has now become a familiar sight on the streets of many cities and towns worldwide. For over 100 years it has run mission halls (called **citadels**), soup-kitchens, hostels for the unemployed and a rescue agency for people who have left home. In Britian and overseas, the Salvation Army is quick to respond to homelessness, natural disasters and local and national emergencies.

Christianity in the community

Whilst in most denominations, traditional worship is the most important way of practising the faith, much of today's Christian activity goes on outside church buildings. Amongst other places, the message is now put over in coffee bars, beach missions and large Christian arts and music festivals. The largest of these festivals, Greenbelt, attracts 25,000 visitors each year.

The Church overseas

In many countries of the world members of the Christian Church are allowed to worship freely. In others their freedom is severely restricted. In most parts of North Africa, for example, the Church is not allowed to make new converts, whilst in other parts, particularly in Central and West Africa, the situation is very different. Today there are around 150 million Christians in this area alone, with new churches springing up frequently. Many of these, however, do not belong to the main denominations.

Why do you think many Christians who have moved to Britain have formed their own churches?

The same is true of many countries in South and Central America. The new churches there worship God in ways which make their members feel at home – with dancing, clapping, chanting and swaying being essential parts of worship. In this part of the world many priests identify themselves with the poor and needy. Some become involved politically and lead protests against those people who exploit them.

In the USA, church-going is much more widespread than it is in Britain, where only one in ten people go to church on Sunday. In the USA it is five times as high. One interesting difference between the two countries is that in America Sunday Schools are not just for children but for the whole family.

Words to remember

Citadel A Salvation Army place of worship.

Salvation Army A Protestant organisation begun in the nineteenth century by William and Catherine Booth.

Do you know

◇ what kind of help organisations like the London City Mission and the Salvation Army bring to those in need?

◇ some of the ways in which the Christian message is being put over today?

◇ one of the main differences between church life in the USA and in Britian?

Things to do

1 Some years ago the Church of England appointed a vicar to find out why fewer and fewer people were going to church in inner-city areas. Imagine that you have just become the vicar of one such church in the centre of a large city. When you arrive, the average number in your Sunday congregation is just twenty. How would you set about attracting people to your church? What types of events would you organise? Would you lay on anything special for young people?

2 Find out all that you can about the work of the Salvation Army. In particular, try to find the answers to the following questions:

a Why do members of the Salvation Army wear their distinctive uniform and why is this organisation called an army?

b What is it that attracts many people to the Salvation Army?

c What is the Salvation Army doing in your area?

d Try to find examples of disasters where the Salvation Army was actively involved, bringing help and comfort.

Why do the holy books matter?

Each of the world's great religions has its own holy scriptures. These are books that are believed to contain God's message. They have been carefully preserved over the centuries and are treated with great respect.

Writing the scriptures

Some of the holy scriptures took a very long time to write down. The **Bible**, for instance, took almost 1,500 years to record, although the New Testament was written in less than 100 years. Most, however, took a shorter time.

The followers of each religion believe that their scriptures alone have come directly from God. They are often called the 'Word of God'. To Muslims, for example, the **Qur'an** (see picture A) is the perfect record of the revelations given by God to the Prophet Muhammad. The Prophet passed on these revelations during his lifetime and his followers wrote them down after he died.

A

Why do you think a Muslim would claim that the Qur'an contains words actually spoken by God?

Respecting the holy books

As the scriptures are believed to be the holy word of God, they are treated with the greatest respect. In a Sikh temple, called a **gurdwara**, for example, the **Guru Granth Sahib** is carried above the head to show that it is 'higher' than any human being. Similarly, when the scrolls of

the Jewish **Torah** are taken out of the **Ark** in a **synagogue**, men try to kiss them as they pass.

When it is being read in public, the Torah is treated in a special way to underline its importance. A metal finger is used so that the reader does not lose his place in the Hebrew text and yet does not touch the scroll with his fingers.

B

These scrolls are a very sacred part of Jewish life. Where are they kept when they are not being read in the synagogue?

The teaching in the scriptures

For every religious believer the most important aspect of their scriptures is the teaching that they contain. As in the past, believers today expect to hear God speaking through these holy books. They look to the words for guidance in shaping their lives. The Sikh faith provides a good example of this. Before taking any important decision, a family reads the Guru Granth Sahib aloud for 48 hours to allow God to speak to them (called **Akhand Path**).

Words to remember

Akhand Path   A continuous reading of the Sikh scriptures to mark an important event or before taking a major decision.

Ark   The cupboard in a synagogue in which the scrolls of the Torah are kept.

Bible   The Christian holy book. It is in two parts – the Old Testament which includes the Jewish sacred scriptures, and the New Testament which documents the life and teaching of Jesus.

Gurdwara   A Sikh place of worship, meaning literally 'the doorway to the Guru'.

Guru Granth Sahib   The Sikh holy book, which was first compiled by Guru Arjan. It is also called the Adi Granth.

Qur'an   The Muslim holy book, which records the revelations given to Muhammad by God.

Synagogue   The place where Jews meet for worship, study and social activity.

Torah   The first five books of the Jewish scriptures, which contain the law and teaching.

Do you know

◇ Why religious believers often refer to their scriptures as the 'Word of God'?
◇ how worshippers show their respect for the Guru Granth Sahib and the Torah?
◇ why the teaching of the holy books is their most important aspect?

Things to do

1 Hidden in this word square are four words or phrases which are in this chapter. Find them and, in a sentence, explain what each of them means. (The words can read across or down.)

```
E P D R U X A L Q I P H K A J
L N E W T E S T A M E N T H L
M O Z U N N K U E L N D J R C
G U R U G R A N T H S A H I B
W L A K I J E A O E M T S S I
B L C I Y J I K K N N O R L L
L A R Z N Q U R A N S R K M L
Z H P X O P D V H U Z A Q E N
C H Y F R T O M J H C H Z X E
```

2 Using the words below, in your book write out and complete the following sentences to show how important the holy books are to worshippers.

a Believers in many religions often call their scriptures the ___ of ___ .

b In a gurdwara, the ___ ___ ___ is always carried above the heads of the worshippers.

c As the scrolls of the ___ are carried past, Jewish men try to ___ them.

d Religious people try to obey the ___ of their holy books.
Torah • word • Guru Granth Sahib • teaching • kiss • God

3 This man is reading the Guru Granth Sahib.

a In which religion is this the holy book?

b Write three sentences about the Guru Granth Sahib and how it is treated.

What are the Jewish scriptures?

The **Tenakh** or Jewish Bible is the name given to the Jewish holy books. ('Bible' comes from the Greek word meaning 'books'.) It is a collection of scriptures written in Hebrew by many different authors over a very long period of time. The same books form the Old Testament in the Christian Bible. Originally the Tenakh was written on parchment in scrolls and that is still how the Torah, the first five books, and the most sacred part to Jews, is preserved today. Each scroll is copied out by hand by a **scribe** and must be perfect. A single mistake and the scroll is destroyed and the work begun again.

The divisions of the scriptures

The Jewish Bible is divided into three parts:

◆ The Torah (The Five Books of Moses). This is made up of the first five books of the Bible – Genesis, Exodus, Leviticus, Deuteronomy and Numbers. They contain the Jewish law given to **Moses** and are the holiest part of the scriptures for Jews. This collection of books tells the story of how the ancient Israelite nation spent over 400 years in Egyptian slavery before being delivered by God through Moses. The account ends 40 years later with the people entering the Promised Land of Canaan. It was during the journey from Egypt to Canaan (called the **Exodus**) that Israel received its laws from God on Mount Sinai including the **Ten Sayings**. These laws are at the heart of the Torah. Jews today still try to follow the laws as the basis for their daily lives.

◆ The Nevi'im (The Books of the Prophets). The **prophets** were men and women who spoke to the people on God's behalf. These books contain moral and religious teachings as well as an account of the earliest period of Jewish history. Amongst the most important prophets to have their words recorded were Isaiah, Jeremiah and Ezekiel. Although the prophets sometimes spoke of future events they were much more concerned that people should live in a way that showed respect to God.

◆ The Ketuvim (The Holy Writings). This is a varied collection of poetry, proverbs and other writings by such people as David and Solomon. Like the Nevi'im, Jews regard these books as holy but not as sacred as the Torah.

Taking care of the scrolls

When a new scroll is presented to a synagogue, a special ceremony takes place. It is then put in the Ark with the other scrolls after it has been 'dressed' and capped by a silver crown. During services, the scrolls are brought out of the Ark and carried in procession to the bimah (a raised platform). The scrolls are then 'undressed' and the relevant part is read. At the end of their useful life, scrolls are not destroyed but are buried in a grave.

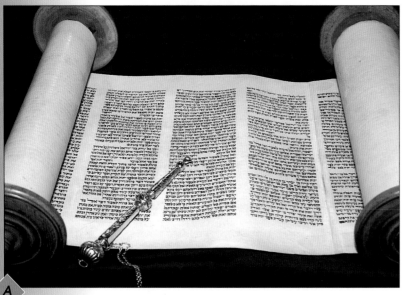

A The Torah scroll is unfurled in a synagogue. Who has been responsible for making this scroll, and why is it such an important job?

Do you know

◇ which three parts the Jewish scriptures are divided into?
◇ where the Torah scrolls are kept in the synagogue?
◇ how Jewish people show their respect for the Torah?

Words to remember

Exodus The name given to the journey that the Israelites took out of Egyptian slavery, and also to the second book in the Bible which records that journey.

Moses The great leader, prophet and law-giver of the Israelites at the time when the Jews left their life of slavery in Egypt and travelled to the Promised Land.

Prophet A person with whom God communicated. The words of many of the prophets are written in the scriptures, although there were a great number whose sayings were not recorded.

Scribe In biblical times this was an expert in the Jewish law, now his main task is to copy out the ancient scriptures by hand.

Tenakh The books of the Jewish Bible in three sections. The word is formed from the initial letters of each part (Torah; Nevi'im; Ketuvim).

Ten Sayings The ten special laws given by God to Moses on Mount Sinai, known to Christians as the Ten Commandments.

Things to do

1 In 132 CE the Roman emperor, Hadrian, forbade all Jews to study or teach the Torah. Rabbi Akiva refused to do what he was told. He said:

> 'A fox once called the fishes in a stream to come ashore and escape from the big fish that preyed on them. They told him that water was their life-element; if they left it they would surely die. If they stayed some might die but the rest would live.'

Akiva went on to explain what he meant:

> 'The Torah is our element of life. Some of us may perish in the trials of these days but as long as there is Torah the people will live.'

In Akiva's parable who or what do you think:
a is the fox?
b are the fishes in the stream?
c is the water?

2 Copy out this crossword and fill in the answers. See how many you can do without looking through this chapter.

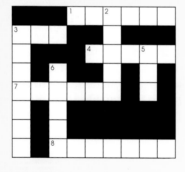

Across
1 The language in which the Jewish Scriptures were written (6)
3 He gave Israel its laws on Mount Sinai (3)
4 The first five books of the Jewish Scriptures are called this (5)
7 The journey of the Israelites out of slavery (6)
8 Stored in the Ark in the synagogue (7)

Down
2 The word 'Bible' means this in Greek (5)
3 The first book in the Tenakh (7)
5 The scrolls of the Torah are kept in this (3)
6 He led the Israelites out of Egypt (5)

What is the Qur'an?

The Qur'an is the holy book for all Muslims. The name comes from the Arabic for 'that which is read or recited' and contains the revelations from **Allah** to the Prophet **Muhammad** by the Angel Jibril (Gabriel).

Putting the Qur'an together

Muslims believe there are two perfect copies of the Qur'an. The first is in heaven and the other is the one that Muhammad's companions put together. It was written in three stages:

◆ During many revelations, the Angel Jibril told Muhammad about the will and mind of Allah.

◆ For many years afterwards, Muhammad was followed around by a growing band of companions. They made a note of the revelations as he told them by writing them down on scraps of stone, pieces of palm branches or whatever was to hand.

◆ A few years after Muhammad's death, his friends decided to bring all this material together into a permanent record. Four copies of the Qur'an were made and sent to cities in which there were many Muslim converts.

The words of the Qur'an

The words of the Qur'an have never been changed since they were first revealed. This is why each copy of the holy book is carefully transcribed (copied out) and then illustrated with great care by hand, as in picture A. The language of the Qur'an is Arabic and it sounds particularly beautiful when read aloud. The text itself is read from right to left with the reader starting at the top right-hand corner.

Although the Qur'an has now been translated into many languages, worshippers still try to learn it in the original language. They start to do this at the age of four when they begin to

---

What the Qur'an means

The Qur'an provides Muslims with a guide for their daily lives. Here are four quotations from it.

a 'Children of Allah, wear your best clothes at every time of worship.'

b 'You who believe, whenever you intend to pray, wash your faces and your hands up to the elbows, and wipe your head and wash your feet up to the ankles.'

c 'You who believe, liquor and gambling, idols and raffles are only a work of Satan, avoid them that you may prosper.'

d 'God has permitted trading and forbidden taking interest.'

◇ Put these verses into your own words and try to explain what you think they mean.

◇ The verses mention several things that a Muslim must and must not do. Make a list of them in your book.

A
This is a page from an old copy of the Qur'an. What do you notice about it?

attend special schools in the mosque – called **madrassah**. The children also learn here how to carry out Muslim practices and the general principles of Islam.

In total the Qur'an has over 6,000 verses. A verse is called an **ayah** or 'sign'. These are divided up into chapters or **surahs** which mean 'steps up' and each chapter has its own title. The title describes the most important theme contained in the surah.

Treating the Qur'an with respect

Muslims treat the Qur'an with the greatest possible respect. Before reading it they wash themselves thoroughly. They then unwrap the holy book from its cover, read the passage and then replace the book carefully on a shelf. It is very important that the Qur'an should always be stored higher than any other book. While it is being read, people do not eat or drink or behave in any way that is disrespectful.

B
Why do you think that Muslims start teaching children about their faith at a very early age?

Do you know ?

◇ what the word Qur'an means and why it has been given this name?
◇ how the Qur'an came to be written?
◇ how Muslims show respect for the Qur'an?

Words to remember

Allah   God in the Muslim religion.

Ayah   A verse of the Qur'an.

Madrassah   A school attached to a mosque; place where Muslim children learn about the Qur'an and the Arabic language.

Muhammad· The name of the final prophet chosen by Allah to receive the Qur'an.

Surah   One of the 114 chapters in the Qur'an.

Things to do

1 Here is a verse from the Qur'an. Copy it into your book and then explain why Muslims are not allowed to question where the Qur'an comes from:

'This Qur'an could not have been composed by any but Allah... It is beyond doubt from the Lord of Creation. If they say, "It is your own invention" say "Compose one chapter like it."'

2 According to Muslim tradition, Muhammad's companions recorded the Qur'an from:

'scraps of parchment and leather, tablets of stone, ribs of palm branches, camels' shoulder blades and ribs, pieces of board and the breasts of men.'

Most of the things in this quotation are things you could write on but how do you think the followers got teachings from 'the breasts of men'?

What are the Hindu scriptures?

There are many Hindu holy books which are divided into two groups:

◆ The **Shruti** ('what is heard'). The Shruti is the four **Vedas**, including the Upanishads which explain the teachings of the Vedas. They are the oldest known books. The word Veda means knowledge and Hindus believe them to have come directly from God himself. Revealed originally to the holy men of India, the Vedas have been passed down from teacher to pupil for centuries. The **Rig Veda**, the most important of the Hindu scriptures, contains 1,028 hymns to various Hindu gods.

◆ The **Smriti** ('what is remembered'). These are the holy writings other than the Vedas which Hindus have remembered and passed on from generation to generation. Some Hindus believe Smriti to be less important than Shruti; others consider them equally important.

The Mahabharata

The **Purana** and the **Itihasa** are part of the Smriti scriptures and tell stories from Hindu legend and history. Amongst them is the **Mahabharata** – the oldest and longest poem in any language. Picture A shows an illustration from one version of it. It has 3,000,000 words and tells the story of two sets of royal cousins who quarrel over who should succeed to the throne. Finally they go to war. Arjuna, one of the cousins, hates fighting but is an excellent warrior.

In the final battle he hesitates because he does not want to kill members of his own family and so he orders his chariot-driver to withdraw from the battle. Arjuna is very surprised when his driver begins to argue with him. Then he realises that his driver is none other than the god **Krishna**, who has come to live on earth. Krishna tells Arjuna that those who die in battle are not dead for ever. The prince believes him and leads his forces to victory.

The Mahabharata also includes the very ancient Bhagavad Gita – The Song of the Lord. Spoken by Krishna, this is the most important scripture for Hindus. An illustration from this holy book is shown opposite.

The Ramayana

The **Ramayana** is another great Hindu epic poem. It tells the story of Rama, a god, who visits the earth and marries Princess Sita. She is then abducted by Ravana, a fierce demon, and taken to the island of Lanka. After fierce fighting, Rama rescues her and they are restored to their thrones.

The theme of both the Mahabharata and the Ramayana is also the basis for most stories in the Hindu scriptures – that good will always triumph over evil, even though evil often appears to be winning.

A In this illustration from the Mahabharata, Krishna is seen as the chariot-driver of Arjuna. Who were Krishna and Arjuna?

Words to remember

Itihasa   A holy book which contains stories from Hindu myth and history.

Krishna   One of the most popular Hindu gods who has visited the earth nine times.

Mahabharata   The longest Hindu epic poem containing almost 1,000,000 verses.

Purana   A holy book which contains many of the well-known stories of Hinduism.

Ramayana   One of the oldest epic poems in Hindu religion, telling the story of Rama and Sita. It has 24,000 verses.

Rig Veda   The most sacred of the Hindu scriptures.

Shruti   The Hindu holy books, including the four Vedas, in which God is believed to have spoken directly to human beings.

Smriti   Hindu scriptures, other than the Vedas, which have been written down from memory.

Vedas   The oldest of the Hindu holy books, collected between 1500 BCE and 800 BCE.

The Laws of Manu

The 'Laws of Manu' is an ancient Hindu book, written between 200 and 100 BCE. Here is an extract:

'Coveting [wanting] the property of others, thinking in one's heart of what is undesirable, and adherence [sticking] to false doctrines [beliefs] are three kinds of sinful mental action. Abusing others, speaking untruth, detracting from the merits of all men and talking idly shall be four kinds of evil verbal action.'

◇ Try to put this into everyday English.
◇ Give examples from your own experience of:
 – 'speaking untruth'
 – 'detracting from the merits of all men'
 – 'talking idly'.

Do you know

◇ which is the most important group of Hindu scriptures?
◇ which is the longest Hindu poem and what it is about?
◇ what the Ramayana and the Mahabharata are about?

Things to do

1 Match up the words in the left-hand column with their correct meaning from the right-hand column:

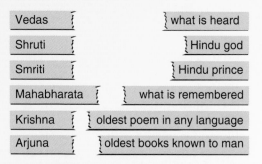

Vedas	what is heard
Shruti	Hindu god
Smriti	Hindu prince
Mahabharata	what is remembered
Krishna	oldest poem in any language
Arjuna	oldest books known to man

2 This picture shows a scene from the Bhagavad Gita, a greatly respected Hindu scripture. Using the information that you are given in this chapter, describe in your own words what the picture shows.

3 Draw a picture or write a story which shows your own idea of good triumphing over evil.

What is the Guru Granth Sahib?

In 1604, Guru Arjan collected together the teachings of the four **Gurus** who came before him and combined them with material from many Hindu and Muslim holy men to form the **Adi Granth**. This illustrates the Sikh belief that truth is not to be found only in one religion since there are many paths to God.

The Guru Granth Sahib

Shortly before he died, in 1708, the tenth and last of the human Gurus, Guru Gobind Singh, added the writings of his father, Guru Tegh Bahadur, to the Adi Granth to form the Guru Granth Sahib.

He also told the Sikhs that there were going to be no more human Gurus (spiritual teachers) to lead them. From now on their only Guru would be the Guru Granth Sahib. Since then, this holy book has been at the centre of every act of worship and is treated with great reverence and respect. For any building to be recognised as a gurdwara (a Sikh place of worship), it must contain a copy of the holy book.

When young babies are brought into the gurdwara a random reading of the Guru Granth Sahib provides the first letter of the baby's name. Marriages are performed in front of the holy book and before a family moves into a new home it is put into the new dwelling for an hour or so.

A

The Guru Granth Sahib is being read in the gurdwara. Do you know which language it is written in and why?

Showing respect

The Guru Granth Sahib is so respected that any Sikh who is going to come into contact with it must take a bath and wash his hands before turning its holy pages. For a long time Sikhs resisted all attempts to have copies of their holy book printed. This was because they did not want it sold through bookshops and so handled casually by non-Sikhs. When a copy of the Guru Granth Sahib is printed it must be an exact copy of the original. Each page must have the same number of words and the book as a whole must have 1,430 pages.

The Mool Mantar

The most important passage in the Guru Granth Sahib comes at the beginning. It is the Sikh creed or statement of belief – the **Mool Mantar**. It can be translated as:

'There is but one God. Truth by name, the creator, the all-pervading spirit, without fear, without enmity. Whose existence is unaffected by time, who does not take birth, self-existent, who is to be realised through his grace.'

The creed is written in Punjabi, the language in which the Sikh scriptures are printed.

Words to remember

Adi Granth   The original Sikh holy book, expanded later to form the Guru Granth Sahib.

Guru   A holy man or teacher. In Sikhism this title is reserved for the ten human Gurus and the Guru Granth Sahib.

Mool Mantar   The Sikh statement of belief taken from the opening of the Guru Granth Sahib.

Do you know

◇ who compiled the Adi Granth?
◇ what is the difference between the Adi Granth and the Guru Granth Sahib?
◇ how the Guru Granth Sahib is treated by Sikhs?

Things to do

1. Look at the picture above. Try to find out:
   a the name of this official in the gurdwara.
   b the name of the fan that he is waving.
   c what the fan is made of.
   d why he is waving the fan.

2. Sikhs believe that wherever the Guru Granth Sahib is found, there is a gurdwara. Picture A shows this holy book being read in the gurdwara. Describe, in your own words, three ways in which Sikhs show great respect towards their holy book.

3. It has been said that Sikhs honour the Guru Granth Sahib without actually worshipping it. What do you think this means?

4. Look carefully at the translation of the Mool Mantar opposite. It contains ten statements about God. Make a list of them. What do you think is meant by each of the following:
   a 'all-pervading spirit'
   b 'Whose existence is unaffected by time'
   c 'who does not take birth'
   d 'self-existent'
   e 'who is to be realised through his grace'?

You might need your teacher's help with one or two of these phrases.

What are the Buddhist holy books?

It was not until 500 years after the death of the **Buddha** in 483 BCE that his teachings were written down. In those days people were used to keeping information alive by word of mouth. However, to make sure that everyone agreed on just what he had said, a meeting of monks listened to all the teachings of the Buddha being recited by two of his closest followers. During the time that nothing was written down, Buddhists held meetings frequently to make sure that the memory of the teaching was still reliable. It was too important for any mistakes to be made.

The Pali and the Sanskrit Canons

Eventually two collections of the Buddha's teachings were made. They are called the Pali **Canon** and the Sanskrit Canon, after the two ancient languages in which they were first written.

- The Pali Canon was the first to be compiled and was written in an Indian language by people in Sri Lanka. This took place in about 30 BCE. The Pali Canon is the most important collection of writings for Theravada Buddhists.

- The Sanskrit Canon was written in the ancient language of India and is widely used amongst Buddhists of the Mahayana tradition.

The Three Baskets

The Buddhist scriptures consist of a threefold collection of texts called the **Tipitaka** – the three baskets. They were probably called 'baskets' because the teachings were first written down on palm leaves which were stored in baskets.

- The first of the three collections is made up of rules of discipline for Buddhist monks and nuns.

- The second of the three collections contains the actual teachings of the Buddha. It is called the Suttaka Pitaka, with sutta meaning 'teaching'. This collection is widely read as it is an important account of what the Buddha said and did. The teachings are called **Dhamma** and the most well-known of these texts is the **Dhammapada** (see the information box).

- The third collection is an explanation of the Buddha's teaching.

The Mahayana scriptures

Both Theravada and Mahayana Buddhists follow the teachings of the Tipitaka but they disagree over which is the most important. For Mahayana Buddhists, the Diamond Sutta and the Lotus Sutta are two of the most important parts. They also have their own holy books.

A

These Buddhist scriptures are written in Sanskrit. Which tradition do they come from and who originally wrote them?

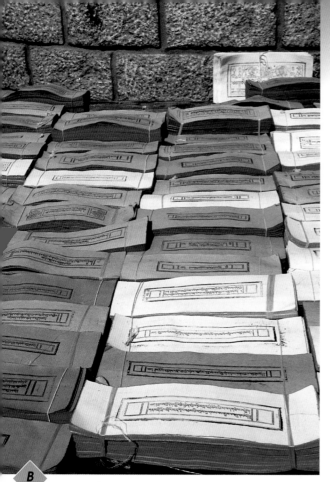

B This shows the Buddhist holy books. What are the differences between the Pali and Sanskrit Canons?

Do you know

- how the teaching of the Buddha was kept alive for 500 years after his death, before it was written down?
- the name given to the basket which contains the Buddha's teachings?
- what the Tipitaka is?

The Dhammapada

The Dhammapada is a collection of the Buddha's sayings and teachings. Here is an extract:

'As the arrow-maker whittles
They tremble, they are unsteady,
And makes straight his arrows
They wander at their will
So the master directs
It is good to control them
His straying thoughts.
And to master them brings happiness.'

- How does the master (the spiritual teacher) direct his thoughts?
- What happens to our thoughts if we do not control them?
- How can a person find happiness?

Things to do

1 Why were the holy books of Buddhism written down? In what way were the teachings of the Buddha kept alive before collections were made?

2 What is a 'sutta'? Why do you think that Mahayana Buddhist have called two of the suttas the 'Diamond Sutta' and the 'Lotus Sutta?'

3 Explain:
a why the Tipitaka is so called.
b what is contained in the Tipitaka.
c what is the most important part of the Tipitaka.

What is the Bible?

The success of the Christian Bible as a book is very impressive. Since 1800 over 3,000,000,000 copies have been printed and, each year, a further 10,000,000 copies are added to the total. Although the **Authorised Version** of the Bible, first published in 1611, remains popular, it has been overtaken in recent years by more modern versions such as *The Good News Bible*, the *New International Version* and the *Revised English Bible*.

The Old and New Testaments

The Christian Bible is divided into two parts:

◆ The Old Testament. This contains 39 books and forms the sacred scriptures, or Tenakh (see page 22), for Jews. The books of the Old Testament cover a time-span of at least 1,000 years and it is not known who wrote many of them. They form the background to much of what is in the New Testament, since nearly all the early Christians were Jews and so were familiar with the Jewish scriptures and their teachings.

◆ The New Testament. This part of the Bible is mainly concerned with Jesus of Nazareth – the Messiah – whose coming into the world was prophesied in the Old Testament. In the New Testament there are two main kinds of writing:

  a History. This includes the four Gospels – by Matthew, Mark, Luke and John – which describe the life and teaching of Jesus. The Gospels of Matthew, Mark and Luke have a similar way of presenting the life of Jesus and so are called **Synoptic Gospels** ('seeing together'). The fourth Gospel, by St John, is very different and was written later. Luke, a doctor, not only wrote one of the Gospels but also the Acts of the Apostles (see pages 6–7). This tells the story of the early days of the Christian Church after Jesus had left the earth.

  b Letters or **Epistles**. There are many of these in the New Testament, written to help and guide the early Christians. Most were written by Paul, although letters are also included by John and Peter.

Inspiration

What binds all of these writers and their very different books together in the Bible? To Christians the Bible is unlike any other book. They believe that the writers were inspired by God and so the books that they have left behind carry an authority that no other writings have.

A
Why do you think that there is a need to have so many different versions of the bible?

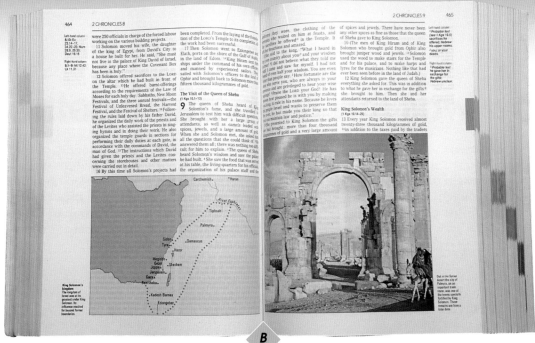

Pages taken from the *Good News Bible*. What do you think makes this Bible different from other versions?

Words to remember

Authorised Version   A version of the Bible completed by a team of scholars in 1611. A copy was placed in every church in England by King James I.

Epistles   Letters in the New Testament written by Paul, Peter, John and others.

Synoptic Gospels   The first three Gospels which present the life and teaching of Jesus in a similar way.

Do you know

◇ which part of the Bible Christians share with Jews?
◇ what the two parts of the Bible are called and one difference between them?
◇ which two kinds of writing go to make up the New Testament?

Things to do

1 These verses refer to the Old Testament teachings, but they sum up how Christians feel about the Bible as a whole:

'We know that what the scripture says is true for ever...'

(John 10.35, from the Good News Bible *Bible Society/Collins, 1994)*

'For the word of God is living and active. Sharper than any double-edged sword, it penetrates even to dividing soul and spirit, joints and marrow; it judges the thoughts and attitudes of the heart.'

(Hebrews 4.12)

a Which word is used here to refer to the writings of the Old Testament?
b What is described as being 'living and active'? What does this phrase suggest to you about the Old Testament?

2 The Bible appears in the *Guinness Book of Records* as the most widely published book of all time. However, it has been said that:

'The Bible is the most widely published book of all time yet it is the least read book in the world.'

a Do you think that this is right?
b If so, why do you think that the Bible is not read more widely?

How was the Bible put together?

Many of the passages in the Bible began life as stories which were kept alive for centuries as people passed them on by word of mouth. In the re-telling, though, it is likely that some details in the stories changed.

Recording information

As time went on, people began to record important events and information to make sure that they were not forgotten. When, for example, Moses received the Ten Commandments on Mount Sinai (see page 22) they are said to have been written on 'tablets of stone' which were then stored, along with other holy objects, in a sacred box called the Ark. The ancient Jews took this box with them wherever they went.

During the main period of Jewish prophecy, the words of many of the prophets were written down by their disciples. Jeremiah, one of the most important prophets, had his own secretary, Baruch, who recorded everything he said. At about the same time **psalms** were written down for use in worship in the **Temple**. They were also kept alive because people regularly sang them together.

Collecting the books together

By the time of Jesus, all the books of the Old Testament had been collected together. There was still some debate about one or two of them but the matter was finally settled at a meeting called the Synod of Jamnia in 90 CE. As most of the first Christians were Jews, when they met after Jesus had left the earth, they continued to use the Jewish scriptures in their worship.

At the same time they talked about Jesus and his teaching. They thought that it was particularly important to listen to those who had heard him, especially his disciples. There was a real fear that their memories of Jesus would die with them. To prevent this happening, **Mark** wrote an account of the life of Jesus around 65 CE. This was almost 40 years after Jesus had left the earth. Luke and Matthew followed soon after with their Gospels. John's Gospel came much later.

Each wrote their own record of the life and teaching of Jesus on scrolls similar to those that you can see in picture B. These were not, however, the earliest written Christian documents. Already Paul had written many letters to churches and individual Christians (see page 8). Although he was not a disciple of Jesus, Paul soon became the leader of the early Christians. His letters were read and treasured by the early believers.

Gradually the collection of books grew and they were added to those of the Old Testament. At two councils held in the fourth century, the Church's seal of approval was finally put on those books which now form what is known as the Bible. Since then it has remained unchanged.

A People have always passed on important pieces of information by word of mouth. How reliable do you think this is as a way of keeping information alive?

A

Why do you think that Jews still keep their holy scriptures on scrolls like their ancestors did?

Words to remember

Mark A follower of Jesus, the author of the first Gospel which he wrote around 65 CE.

Psalms Jewish songs sung in the Temple to praise God. Many are contained in the Book of Psalms in the Old Testament.

Temple This means 'house of holiness'. It refers to a very large building in Jerusalem, first built by King Solomon. It was destroyed and rebuilt several times, finally by King Herod. The Romans destroyed it in 70 CE.

Do you know

◇ how the ancient Jews kept, and stored, important pieces of information?
◇ the names of the followers of Jesus who wrote the Gospels in the New Testament?
◇ who wrote the oldest documents in the New Testament?

Things to do

1 Copy out and complete these sentences:

a The Ten Commandments were said to have been given to Moses on Mount Sinai on _____ of _____.

b The _____ was a sacred box in which the Jews stored the Ten Commandments.

c When the followers of Jesus began to die, _____, _____ and _____ wrote down their accounts of his life.

d _____ wrote many letters and these are some of the earliest Christian documents.

e It was not until a meeting in _____ that the composition of the Jewish scriptures was finally settled.

2 The Gospel accounts of the life of Jesus are drawn from information provided by eye-witnesses, especially the disciples. Imagine yourself to have been one of these and describe the impact that the three years you spent with Jesus before he left the earth has had on you. Here are some Bible references that might help you.

◆ Matthew 8.23–7 ◆ John 11.1–44
◆ John 13.12–17

How was the Bible translated into English?

The Old Testament was originally in Hebrew and the New Testament in Greek. Towards the end of the fourth century, a monk called Jerome translated the Bible into Latin. For a long time afterwards, this was the only version used in England, although parts of it were translated into local dialects. More frequently an English translation was written underneath the Latin text. A beautiful example of this is the **Lindisfarne Gospels** which were produced by the monks who lived at Lindisfarne on Holy Island, off the north-east coast of England.

A

The beginning of Mark's Gospel in the Lindisfarne Gospels. Who produced this translation and where?

The Bible in English

In the fourteenth century, the preacher John **Wycliffe** and his followers began to call for the translation of the Bible into English. They argued that only the local priest could read Latin and that as the Bible belonged to the people so they should be able to read it in their own language. His followers, the Lollards, set about translating the Bible and they wrote it out by hand. About 200 copies of their work still exist.

When the first book was printed in 1454, there was a demand to print the Bible but this did not happen until 1526. Even then, it was only the New Testament. This was the work of William **Tyndale** who had to print the book in Germany and smuggle it into England hidden in bales of wool and wine casks. Tyndale had promised that:

> 'A boy who drives the plough in England shall know more of the Bible than many priests.'

The Church in Rome felt that the translating of the Bible into English threatened their power. As a result, Tyndale was burned at the stake in Belgium in 1536.

The English Bible in print

In 1535, Miles Coverdale produced the first printed English Bible. Within three years a copy was placed in every church in England. These Bibles were so valuable that they were chained down to prevent thieves from taking them.

In 1611 the most famous translation of all was printed. It was sponsored by King James I and became known as the Authorised Version. For the next 300 years it stood unchallenged before other translations were made. Even today it is still used on official occasions and in many churches, in spite of the popularity of more modern versions.

Words to remember

Lindisfarne Gospels a very early illustrated translation of the four Gospels in the New Testament produced by monks at Lindisfarne.

Tyndale 1490–1536 English translator of the New Testament, executed for his work.

Wycliffe 1329–84 A preacher opposed to some of the teachings of the Roman Catholic Church and condemned by the Pope.

Do you know

◇ what the Lindisfarne Gospels are?
◇ how John Wycliffe and his followers contributed to the translation of the Bible into English?
◇ what parts were played by William Tyndale and Miles Coverdale in the printing of the Bible in English?

B

John Wycliffe, leader of the Lollards, with some of his followers. Why did he think the Bible should be translated into English?

Things to do

1 In picture A you can see the opening to Mark's Gospel in the Lindisfarne Gospels. The text was illuminated (decorated) with great care.

a Copy out any verse from the Bible and decorate it in the style of the Lindisfarne Gospels.

b William Tyndale, amongst others, was prepared to die in his fight to have the Bible translated into English. Why do you think that he saw his task as being so important?

c Why do you think that such great care has always been taken of the Bible?

2 At the end of the Lindisfarne Gospels, the monks involved in the translation added this note:

'Eadfrith, Bishop of the Church at Lindisfarne, he at the first wrote this book for God and St Cuthbert and for all the saints in common that are in the island, and Ethilwald, Bishop of those of Lindisfarne Island, bound and covered it outwardly as best he could.

At Bilfrith the anchorite [hermit] he wrought as a smith the ornaments that are on the outside, and adorned it with gold and with gems, also with silver overgilded, a treasure without deceit. And Alfred, an unworthy and most miserable priest, with God's help and Cuthbert's, overglossed it in English...'

a What impression do you get from this description about the teamwork that was needed to produce the Lindisfarne Gospels?

b Can you find any clue in the quotation as to who might have written these words?

3 Imagine that you and a friend are involved in the early work of translating the Bible into English. Both the king and the Church are opposed to what you are doing. Describe some of the dangers of your work and the steps you might take to make sure that the Bible is printed and that copies of it reach those who want to read it.

Why were there so many translations of the Bible?

Before 1611, when the Authorised Version of the Bible was published, there had been many different translations. Then, for some 250 years, the work of translating stopped. It was only revived towards the end of the nineteenth century when some very old biblical manuscripts were found. These were much more ancient, and better, than those used by the scholars who produced the Authorised Version.

New translations

In 1844 and 1859, Count Tischendorf, a scholar, made two visits to the monastery of St Catherine on Mount Sinai. Here he was astonished to discover some priceless manuscripts. Amongst them were the oldest to have come to light so far. These have been called **Codex Sinaiticus** and are now in the British Museum in London.

As a result of this discovery, a new translation of the Bible, the **Revised Version**, was published in 1885. However, it was very much like the Authorised Version. It was not until 1903 that Richard Weymouth published the first New Testament in 'everyday English'. Following this, in 1945 J B Phillips, a young Anglican clergyman, found that young people in his church could not understand the Bible. He translated the books of the New Testament into words that they found easier. This translation became very popular and is still used today.

The New English Bible and beyond

In 1961 the New Testament of the **New English Bible** was published, to be followed five years later by the Old Testament. This translation became most popular for reading aloud in church services. In the years that followed a committee of scholars worked on yet another revision and this was finally published in 1989. They called it the **Revised English Bible**.

Nothing, however, could rival the success of the **Good News Bible** published in two parts – the New Testament in 1966 and the Old Testament ten years later. Originally written in America for people who used English as a second language, 8,000,000 copies were sold in the first year of publication. It was at the top of the bestseller lists for months. Today over 80,000,000 copies of this Bible are in circulation. Apart from its easy-to-read text, the great attraction of the *Good News Bible* has been its unusual illustrations.

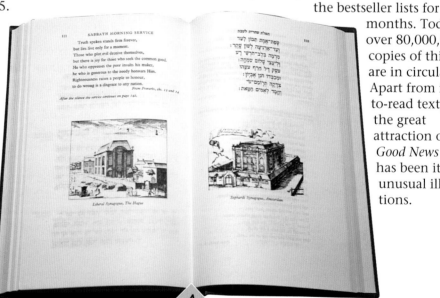

A

This shows the Hebrew text of the Old Testament. Why do you think that, generally speaking, the older the manuscript the more valuable it is?

Do you know

◇ why so many new translations of the Bible have appeared since the Authorised Version?
◇ how Codex Sinaiticus came to light?
◇ which popular translations of the Bible have been published since the Second World War?

Words to remember

Codex Sinaiticus A very old biblical manuscript. A 'codex' is the name for an early form of book made by sewing leaves of writing material together.

Good News Bible A very popular translation, known at first as *Today's English Version*, published in two parts with the New Testament in 1966 and the whole Bible in 1976.

New English Bible This was first produced in 1966.

Revised English Bible Published in 1989, this brought the *New English Bible* up to date.

In this Greek text of the New Testament, an English translation has been added underneath. What do you think are some of the problems that anyone translating the Bible faces?

Revised Version This was published in 1885 and used the same language as the Authorised Version, but contained a few alterations in the light of new manuscripts.

Things to do

These different translations of the same verses from the New Testament (Hebrews 1.1–2) show how the text of the Bible has changed over time:

> 'God in tyme past diversly and in many wayes, spake vnto the fathers by the Prophets: but in these last dayes he hath spoken vnto vs by his sonne, whom he hath made heyre of all things, by whom also he made the worlde.'
>
> *(Tyndale, 1526)*

> 'God, who at sundry times and in divers manners spake in time past unto the fathers by the prophets, hath in these last days spoken to us by his Son, whom he hath appointed heir of all things, by whom also he made the worlds.'
>
> *(Authorised Version, 1611)*

> 'In the past, God spoke to our ancestors many times and in many ways through the prophets, but in these last days he has spoken to us through His Son. He is the one through whom God created the universe, the one whom God has chosen to possess all things at the end.'
>
> *(The Good News Bible, 1976)*

a Do you think that updating the language of the Bible is helpful or not? Give some reasons for your answer.

b Do you think that one version is more suitable to be read in church than any others? If so, what do you think this version should sound like?

c Is it important that the Bible should be in the everyday language of the people? What are the reasons for your answer?

How is the Bible used?

The Bible plays a very important part in the lives of individual Christians as well as being at the centre of their group worship. We can see this in three different ways:

Personal Bible study

Many Christians set aside a time each day when they pray and read the Bible (often called **Quiet Time**). They believe that God speaks to them through the words of the Bible and they spend some time praying beforehand that this will happen. They seek the help of God's Holy Spirit to understand what they are reading.

Many Christians use Bible-study notes to help them find the meaning of Bible passages. If used daily, the notes help them to study the whole Bible in about three years. Picture A shows some of the Bible-reading notes which are specially written to suit children, young people and adults.

Readings during services

Passages from the Bible are read aloud in almost all church services. In the Church of England and the Roman Catholic Church, for example, most services contain three readings:

- an Old Testament reading
- a passage from the Gospels
- a reading from the Epistles.

The passages from the Old Testament and the Epistles can be read by members of the congregation. The one from the Gospels, however, is usually read by a priest. This sometimes takes place in the middle of the church with the Bible being held by a server. This mark of respect emphasises the belief that the reading from the Gospels is central to Christian worship and the most important part of the scriptures.

What do you think that Christians hope to gain from reading the Bible regularly?

A

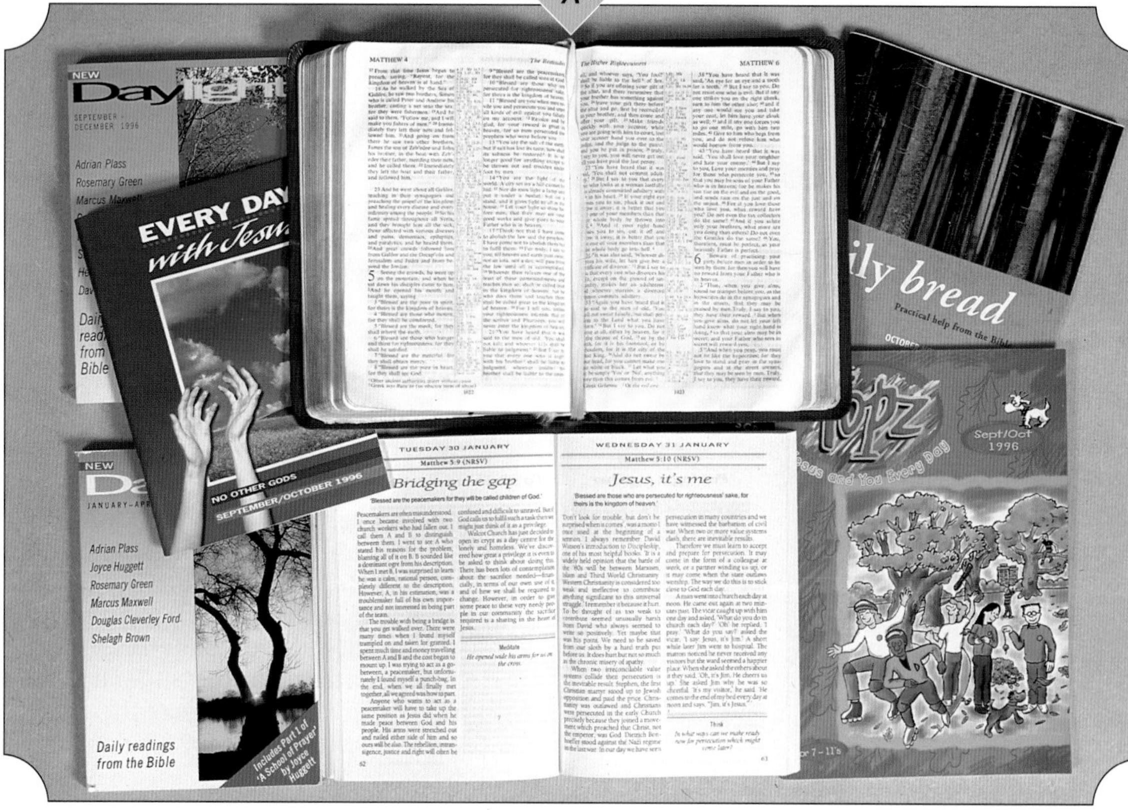

Another important part of a service is the **sermon**. This is when the priest or minister explains a part of the Bible to the congregation. In Nonconformist Churches the sermon is the most important part of the service.

Bible study with others

Many church congregations meet regularly in smaller groups in someone's house. It is at these meetings that a part of the Bible's teaching is discussed. In the Anglican and Roman Catholic Churches the season of **Lent** is an important part of the Church year and a time when many house groups get together. During Lent Christians return to the story of the death and Resurrection of Jesus in the Gospels and spend time thinking, reflecting and praying around it.

Why do you think that meeting and talking about the Bible is a very important part of worship for most Christians?

Do you know

◇ what a Christian means by Quiet Time?
◇ how Christians set out to understand the Bible better?
◇ what part the Bible plays in Christian worship?

Words to remember

Lent A period of six weeks leading up to Easter. Traditionally this is the time when Christians reflect on the events surrounding the death of Jesus.

Quiet Time The part of each day which many Christians set aside to pray and read their Bible.

Sermon The part in the Christian service where the priest or minister explains some part of the Bible to the congregation.

Things to do

Here are two young Christians talking about reading the Bible. Read carefully what they have to say:

'I started reading the Bible when I was 13. I knew nothing about what it had to say and so I was starting from scratch. To begin with I was completely lost but now my Bible reading is a very important part of each day. With the help of God's Holy Spirit I find that I can hear God "speaking" to me through the Bible.'

(Anne, 15)

'I don't find it easy to read the Bible. Finding enough time is the first problem, but even when I do I don't always understand what I'm reading. I always remind myself that the Bible was written a long time ago and for people who lived in a very different world from mine.'

(John, 16)

a You will often hear Christians say that God speaks to them through reading the Bible. What do you think they mean when they say this?
b John refers to some of the problems that he finds when he reads the Bible. Can you think of any problems that people might find when they begin to read the Bible seriously?

What is the Bible all about?

The Bible divides into two parts – the Old Testament which tells the history of the Jewish people, and the New Testament which is about Jesus and the start of the Christian Church.

The history of the Jews

The opening chapters of the first book of the Old Testament, called **Genesis**, raise some very important questions:

◆ how was the universe created and by whom?

◆ where did the first people on earth come from?

◆ what is the relationship between God and human beings?

◆ why did the first people, and all of their descendants, marry?

◆ what is the relationship between human beings and the rest of creation – including the animal world?

◆ why is there **sin** (wrong-doing) in the world?

In story form, the creation of the world by God is described as happening in seven days. The Book of Genesis goes on to say that the first man and woman – Adam and Eve – lived in a perfect garden. Nothing disturbed their perfect world until sin entered. The woman gave in to the temptation of the serpent (snake) and persuaded her husband to do so as well.

People who study religion accept that events in Genesis were unlikely to have occurred as they are told, but rather that the ideas and questions raised behind the stories are true.

God punished the man and the woman for their sin. They were both sent away from the garden. In the harsh new world in which they found themselves, the man had to work hard to provide food for himself and his family. The woman was told that her punishment was to experience great pain every time she gave birth to a baby.

So begins the story that runs through the rest of the Old Testament – of the Jewish people, who were chosen by God. From Adam and Eve descended **Abraham**, the father of the Jewish nation, who made an agreement with God that his descendants would worship God alone. Abraham's grandson, **Jacob**, was renamed 'Israel' and his twelve sons became the fathers of the twelve tribes of Israel.

Throughout the many centuries that followed, the Jews spent much time in slavery. At different times in their history, God sent many leaders to them (among them Moses – see page 22) to lead them out of captivity. Each time, despite their good intentions, God's people failed to live up to the teaching that God gave them and, as a result, lost their homeland and freedom. The Old Testament ends with Israel under Roman control.

A

This drawing illustrates the Jewish and Christian belief that the first man and woman lived in a perfect garden. What do you think might be the truth behind this story?

The life and teaching of Jesus

Then came Jesus. His followers believed that he was God's Son, the Messiah, the chosen leader of the Jews. As an adult he was baptised by John the Baptist in the River Jordan. For a short time Jesus taught his disciples and the people about God before being put to death by the Roman authorities, who saw him as a threat to them. The New Testament scriptures record that shortly after being buried, Jesus was brought back to life by God (the Resurrection). It is belief in this event which is central to Christianity.

Through the Gospels and other writings, the New Testament explains these events to Christian believers. Paul's letters were sent to individual people as well as churches, setting out what it means to be a Christian. Strangely enough, though, Paul and other epistle writers, such as John and Peter, rarely referred to actual events in the life of Jesus.

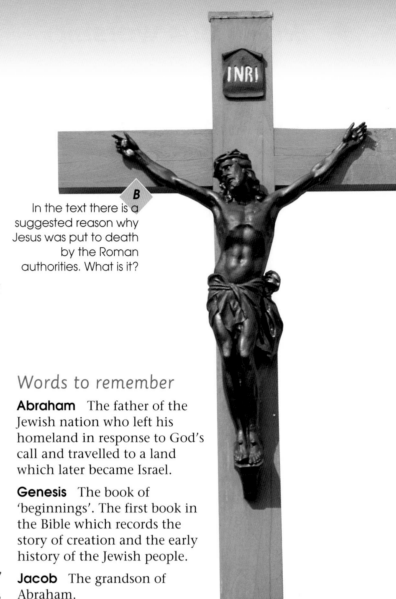

B
In the text there is a suggested reason why Jesus was put to death by the Roman authorities. What is it?

Words to remember

Abraham The father of the Jewish nation who left his homeland in response to God's call and travelled to a land which later became Israel.

Genesis The book of 'beginnings'. The first book in the Bible which records the story of creation and the early history of the Jewish people.

Jacob The grandson of Abraham.

Sin An act of rebellion or dis-obedience against the known will of God.

Do you know

◇ which questions are posed, and answered, by the early chapters of Genesis?
◇ what story runs through the Old Testament?
◇ what happened to Jesus in the New Testament?

Things to do

1 Copy out and complete these sentences:
a _____ is the story of beginnings.
b The Old Testament part of the Bible is the story of a people, the _____, who were chosen by God.
c It was _____ who made an agreement with God that his descendants would worship him.
d _____'s twelve sons became the fathers of the twelve _____ of Israel.
e God sent many people to rescue the Jews from slavery including _____.

f Jesus's followers believed that he was God's _____, the _____.

2 Imagine that you are a Christian with a friend who knows very little about the Bible.
a Which questions do you think your friend might ask you about the Bible?
b How do you think you might answer them?
c What would you say to your friend when he or she asked you to explain what the Bible is all about?

Religious worship

How do Jews worship?

The Jewish **Shabbat**, or Sabbath Day, begins at sunset on Friday and runs through until nightfall on Saturday evening. During this time Jews are forbidden to do any work. Instead they delight in the rest that God has given them. As this quotation from the **Talmud** shows, Shabbat is looked on as one of God's greatest gifts to the Jewish people:

> 'God said to Moses, "I have a precious gift in my treasure house. 'Sabbath' is its name. Go and tell the people of Israel that I wish to give it to them."'

Shabbat worship

On the morning of Shabbat, Jews make their way to the nearest synagogue. Most of them will walk rather than using their car or public transport. The service in the synagogue can only begin when a **minyan** (ten men) are present. In most synagogues men and women are separated, with young children sitting with their mothers in the balcony.

Each person follows the service in their **siddur** (prayer book). One of the most important parts of the service is when the Ark is opened and one of the scrolls of the Torah (the Jewish scriptures) is taken out and carried to the **bimah** (see page 22). It is a great honour to be called up to read from the Torah. In most synagogues it is only men who do this, although in some synagogues women read from the Torah as well. The cover, crown and breastplate are then replaced on the scroll before it is taken back to the Ark.

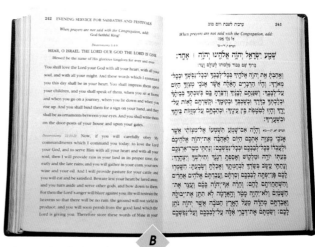

B

In most religions there is a special book which sets out the order of the different services. Why do you think that it is important for everyone to follow the same words in a service?

During the service, psalms (religious songs) are sung by the congregation from the Book of Psalms in the Jewish Bible. No musical instruments can be played on Shabbat since that would involve work so each song is unaccompanied. In larger synagogues there is a song-leader.

Prayers also form an important part of each act of worship. Many are said during the Shabbat service including the **Shema** and the **Amidah**. The Shema is taken directly from Deuteronomy 6.4–9 and is the basic Jewish statement of belief in one God. You can find a copy of this prayer in the information box.

A

In this synagogue you can see a balcony clearly. Why is it there?

44

The Shema

This shows the Shema in Hebrew. In English it says:

'Hear, O Israel: The Lord our God, the Lord is one. Love the Lord your God with all your heart and with all your soul and with all your strength.'

(Deuteronomy 6.4–5)

What does the Shema say about God and what does it say about the way that human beings should respond to him?

Words to remember

Amidah A daily prayer which contains 18 blessings. Some blessings are always said, others differ on weekdays, Sabbaths and festivals.

Bimah A desk or raised platform in a synagogue from where the Torah is read.

Minyan The word means 'count' and refers to the minimum number of men who need to be present before a service can be held in a synagogue.

Shabbat The Sabbath Day, a day of rest which is set aside for prayer and worship. It reminds all Jews that God rested on the seventh day after creating the world in six days.

Shema The word means 'hear'; this is the main Jewish prayer stating a belief in one God.

Siddur The Jewish daily prayer book.

Talmud A book of Jewish laws.

Do you know ?

◇ what a minyan is?
◇ what Shabbat is?
◇ what the Shema and the Amidah are?

Things to do

1 Copy the Shema into your book and learn it. Then answer these questions:
  a What do you think the words 'The Lord our God, the Lord is one' mean?
  b Why do you think the people are told to love God 'with all your heart and with all your soul and with all your might'?

2 The Amidah contains 18 blessings. Here is a short extract:

'O Lord, open my lips and my mouth shall declare your praise. Blessed are you, O Lord our God and God of our Fathers, God of Abraham, God of Isaac and God of Jacob, the great, mighty and revered God, the most high God who bestows loving kindnesses and possesses all things.'

  a Which people from the scriptures are mentioned here? Can you remember anything about them?
  b Make a list of all the things that this extract says about God.

3 A rabbi who lived in the tenth century had this to say about Shabbat:

'The Sabbath is an opportunity to achieve rest from the abundance of one's toil so that one may acquire a little knowledge and pray a little more, and so that people might meet together and discuss matters of Torah...'

According to this rabbi, Shabbat allows a Jew to do five things. What are they?

How do Muslims worship?

In Muslim countries, the **mu'adhin** climbs to the top of the **minaret** five times a day to issue the 'Call to Prayer'. In Britain the same call still goes out but it is usually made from inside the **mosque**. Wherever it is said, though, the words are always the same – see the information box.

Washing

All male Muslims must attend the mosque for prayers at midday on Fridays unless they are ill or travelling in a country where there are no mosques nearby. On entering the mosque they remove their shoes as a sign of respect for Allah. Washing facilities are provided so that people can go through a shared washing ritual (called **wudu** – see picture A). They cleanse their hands, rinse their mouth and nostrils, wash their arms to the elbows, lightly wipe the forehead, ears and neck before washing both feet to the ankles. This is done three times and is very important. It means that the worshipper is both physically and spiritually clean before entering the presence of Allah.

Friday prayers

Once washing is over, the worshipper can enter the prayer hall of the mosque to pray to Allah. The Prophet Muhammad described prayer as:

'a stream into which the faithful worshipper dives five times a day.'

Just as water cleanses the outside of a person's body, so prayer cleanses his soul. The prayers which are said together with other Muslims in the place of worship are thought much more important than someone's personal prayers

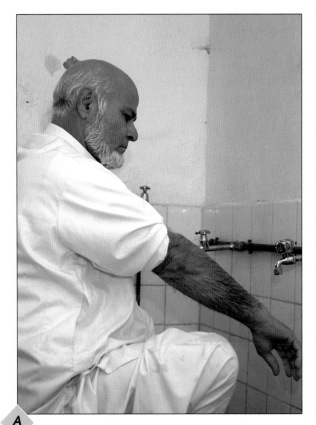

A
Why does a Muslim wash himself thoroughly before entering the mosque to pray?

The Muslim Call to Prayer

'God is the greatest. God is the greatest. God is the greatest. God is the greatest.
I bear witness that there is no God but Allah. I bear witness that there is no God but Allah.
I bear witness that Muhammad is the messenger of Allah. I bear witness that Muhammad is the messenger of Allah.
Come to prayer. Come to prayer.
Come to security. Come to security.
God is the greatest. God is the greatest.
There is no God but Allah.'

◇ What is the Muslim name for God?
◇ Who was God's messenger?
◇ Where should the Muslim go for prayer?
◇ Why do you think that each phrase is repeated at least twice?

The prayers in the mosque are led by the **imam** who takes all worshippers through several **rak'ahs**. During each rak'ah, amongst other actions, a worshipper places his face on the ground twice whilst kneeling to show that he submits himself to Allah. The name of the religion, **Islam**, means 'submission to Allah'.

Praying in a clean place

While Muslims prefer to pray in a mosque – especially during Friday prayers – it is not essential. They can pray to Allah anywhere as long as they are kneeling in a clean place. To guarantee this a **prayer mat** is used. It is often plain coloured and has a pattern with an arch in it. This is pointed in the direction of **Makkah**. All prayer takes place facing the holy city.

Muslim women pray in the same way as men but they do not have to go to the mosque. They have family responsibilities and must not neglect them. They are encouraged, therefore, to say their prayers at home so that they can look after their family at the same time.

Words to remember

Imam   The leader of public prayer; a greatly respected member of the Muslim community.

Islam   This means 'submission', and is the name given to the religion based on the teaching of the Prophet Muhammad.

Makkah   The holy city of Islam in Saudi Arabia, birthplace of the Prophet Muhammad.

Minaret   The tower attached to a mosque, from which the mu'adhin calls the faithful to prayer.

Mosque   The Muslim place of worship.

Mu'adhin   The person who summons Muslims to prayer from the minaret.

Prayer mat   A mat laid on the ground to ensure that the place of prayer is clean.

Rak'ah   The practice of repeating set prayers together with movements of the body.

Wudu   The washing ritual which each Muslim must go through before praying.

What are these Muslims showing as they pray in this position? **B**

Do you know

◇ how often the Call to Prayer is given and what is said?
◇ why washing is such an important part of prayer for a Muslim?
◇ how men's responsibilities with regard to prayer are different from those for women?

Things to do

1 a Do you know of any religions other than Islam which require people either to take off their shoes or cover their heads when they enter a place of worship? If so, which are they?

b What are people showing when they do this?

2 The main emphasis in Muslim worship is upon the greatness and mercy of God and the weakness of human beings.

a How is this underlined in the Muslim approach to prayer?

b Find a copy of the Christian Lord's Prayer and compare it with the Muslim Call to Prayer.

◆ Are the two prayers similar in any way?

◆ Do the two prayers approach God in a similar way?

◆ What are the main differences between the two prayers?

How do Sikhs worship?

On entering a gurdwara, Sikhs remove their shoes and sit cross-legged on the carpeted floor for worship. Each man must wear his **turban** and each woman a **dupatta**. Having bowed low in front of the holy book (the Guru Granth Sahib), they then present their gifts of food or money. If they want to, they can also give a silk cloth to cover the holy book.

A

These gifts are presented in front of the holy book before being distributed to those in need. Why do you think Sikhs do this?

Acts of worship

As there are no priests in Sikhism, anyone – male or female – can conduct a Sikh act of worship. Everyone is equal in the sight of God and so equally capable of leading an act of worship. The service itself can last any length of time between one and five hours. During this time the worshippers are free to come and go as they please, although everyone is expected to be in the gurdwara as the service draws to a close.

The Guru Granth Sahib is kept covered during the service unless someone is reading from it. The **granthi** sits behind the holy book throughout and waves a special fan or **chauri** over it. This fan, traditionally made out of yak hair, is a symbol of royalty and shows the great respect given to the Guru Granth Sahib.

Sikh men and women worship together although they sit separately in the hall. Hymn singing is a very important part of Sikh worship and this is often accompanied by musicians using a harmonium and a pair of small drums. At the end of the service everyone stands and faces the Guru Granth Sahib to listen to the **Ardas**. You can find a short extract from it in the information box.

Finally, **karah parshad** is given to the congregation. This is cooked in the gurdwara kitchen and brought into the hall before the end of the service. It is touched by the **kirpan** before being given out. Eating together is a sign that all people are equal and united in their faith. Eating karah parshad also shows that no one is allowed to leave the Guru Granth Sahib's presence empty-handed.

The Ardas

Here is a short extract from this important Sikh prayer:

'O True King, O Loved Father, we have sung Thy sweet hymns, heard Thy life-giving Word... may these things find a loving place in our hearts and serve to draw our souls towards Thee. Save us, O Father, from lust, wrath, greed, undue attachment and pride... Give us light, give us understanding, so that we may know what pleases Thee. Forgive our sins...'

◇ Which two names are applied to God here?
◇ Which five things does the believer ask God to save him from?
◇ Which three things does the worshipper ask God to do for him?

In the langar

After the service everyone gathers for a communal meal in the **langar**. People sit in rows to eat with the men and women still separate. Everyone stays for this meal which brings together all members of the Sikh community and anyone who might be visiting the gurdwara. It is a good way of breaking down any barriers which there might be between people.

Why do you think that music plays such an important part in many religious services?

Words to remember

Ardas   A prayer which forms a part of most Sikh services.

Chauri   A fan waved over the Guru Granth Sahib during services.

Dupatta   A silk scarf worn in a gurdwara as a head-covering by Sikh women.

Granthi   An official in the gurdwara, whose main task is to read the Guru Granth Sahib in public and perform other religious duties.

Karah parshad   Food shared by the congregation as part of a service. It is a mixture of flour, sugar and ghee (clarified butter).

Kirpan   A short sword, carried by members of the Khalsa (see page 81), used in many Sikh ceremonies. It symbolises resistance to evil.

Langar   The kitchen next to the gurdwara.

Turban   A head-covering worn by Sikh men.

Do you know

◇ which symbols of the Sikh faith men and women wear in the gurdwara?
◇ what are the main features of Sikh worship in the gurdwara?
◇ what happens at the end of a service in the gurdwara and what it represents?

Things to do

1 People often share a meal with friends to celebrate a special occasion like a birthday or a wedding.
   a Write down five other occasions on which people might eat a special meal.
   b Why do you think that friends celebrate a special occasion by eating together?
   c What religions do you know of which include a meal in one of their services?

2 Sikh people do not have a special day for worship, although in Britain most gurdwaras hold their services on Sundays. Why do you think some religions have a special day for worship and others do not?

3 Here is one Sikh describing his weekly visit to the gurdwara:

'Everyone starts by saying the hymns from our Holy Book and ends by joining in a special meal. As we worship God together, our children are allowed to wander around freely just as they like. To be truthful there is a lot of movement throughout the service as people come and go all the time. We are used to this but visitors find it a little strange. The end of the service is the most important time and all of the worshippers are expected to be there for that.'

Which kind of service would you like most to attend – one that was very quiet or one with a lot of movement and noise? Give your reasons why.

How do Hindus worship?

The Hindu approach to public worship is rather different from other religions. Worship at home is far more important than any performed in a temple. As with many other religions, there is a great emphasis upon cleanliness in Hinduism. Each morning starts with a bath since a Hindu cannot say his prayers until his body is clean.

In the temple

After morning cleansing, many Hindus pay a visit to their local temple (see picture A). They can go there with their family or on their own. In the temple, men, women and children all worship together. There is no organised worship with set prayers and hymns, but each person kneels in front of the **shrine** to perform their own **puja**. The form that this takes varies from shrine to shrine but usually involves a worshipper presenting the god or goddess with a gift of sweets or flowers. The priest then gives the worshipper a blessed offering, **prasad**, and makes a mark on their forehead with red powder.

A short time of silence then follows when each worshipper offers up their own silent prayers to God before the sweets that have been placed before the **murti** are returned. The worshipper eats a small part of them before giving what remains to everyone in the temple – rich and poor.

Praying at home

Acts of worship can be performed at any time since there is no special day set aside for worship in Hinduism. As Hindus can worship God anywhere, many of them pay only rare visits to the temple. They prefer to carry out their puja in the home in front of a small shrine. In most Hindu families it is the mother's responsibility to make sure that offerings are made regularly to the god at home. She also teaches the children in her family about their religious responsibilities.

At the same time temples do play an important social as well as a religious part in Hindu life. At the moment there are only a few Hindu temples in Britain, although some Hindu groups are now either building their own or converting existing buildings. The newest purpose-built temple has recently been opened in North London.

A

What do you notice that is distinctive about this Hindu place of worship?

Do you know

◇ where most Hindu worship takes place?
◇ what a puja is?
◇ what a Hindu offers to the god or goddess when he or she visits a temple?

Words to remember

Murti An image or deity used as a focus of worship.

Prasad An offering given to a Hindu by a priest.

Puja An act of worship carried out by a Hindu in a temple or at home.

Shrine A holy building, structure or place.

This picture shows Hindus at a shrine. What do you think prayer really is?

B

Things to do

1 Write out and complete these sentences using the information in this chapter:

  a _____ and _____ are often presented as offerings to the Hindu gods.

  b The priest presents each worshipper with a _____ _____ which is also called a _____.

  c Before an act of worship in a temple each Hindu must _____ thoroughly.

  d A puja is performed in front of the _____.

  e After giving them an offering, a priest makes a _____ on the _____ of each worshipper with _____ _____.

2 Many Hindus in Britain do not attend a temple regularly. Here is one young Hindu girl describing a visit which she had recently made to India:

  'When I was in India a few weeks ago, my parents took me to see many Hindu temples but I wasn't too sure what to make of them. My mum told me that if we still lived in India, we would visit a temple every day to say our prayers. That is the custom there. In this country [Britain], however, things are very different. We do not have a temple anywhere near to where we live and so we just pray to God wherever we might be – in the house or in the open air.'

  a Do you think that a young Hindu might find it difficult to practise their religion without going anywhere near a temple?

  b What do you think would be the advantages to a young believer of meeting regularly with other Hindus?

3 This person is standing before a murti in a shrine in their own home. Why do you think that worshipping at home is so important to a Hindu?

51

5

What are churches like?

Some Christians do not think that the place in which they worship God is particularly important. They are just as happy meeting in a community centre or someone's home as in a church. Others – like the Plymouth Brethren and the Quakers – try to keep their places of worship as simple as possible. The majority of Christians, however, attach great importance to the building in which they worship God. They regard it as a sacred place with an atmosphere which makes them aware of God's presence.

Places of worship

Although Christian churches vary a great deal in their design and age, most of them have certain things in common:

◆ The **altar**. In many churches, particularly Anglican, Roman Catholic and Orthodox ones, this is the focal point at the east end of the church. Here services are conducted and the **Eucharist** is celebrated. People facing the altar are looking in the direction of the rising sun and this has long symbolised the rising of Jesus from the dead.

◆ The **pulpit**. Most churches have a pulpit from where the sermon is given during worship. The sermon is particularly important in Nonconformist services. The pulpit is the focal point in churches which do not have an altar (see picture B).

◆ The shape of the building. The church itself (particularly older buildings) may be in the shape of a cross as a reminder of Jesus's death.

◆ Stained-glass windows. These often tell stories from the Bible and of the saints. In the past they were an important way of teaching people who could not read the Bible for themselves.

◆ The **font**. Many churches have a font which holds the water that is used to baptise babies. In older churches this stands just inside the door to remind people that baptism is the 'door' through which people must pass to become members of the Christian Church.

◆ Churches are often places of great beauty and peace. This is particularly true of **cathedrals** which are works of art in themselves. For centuries people have believed that beautiful churches help them to worship God better.

A

What kind of atmosphere do you think you might feel as you entered this church?

B

What does the pulpit in a Baptist church tell you about the importance of preaching in this denomination?

In addition, churches of the different denominations (see pages 16–17) have their own individual features. For example, Baptist churches have a baptistry for adult baptism at the front of a church. Roman Catholic churches have a **confessional** so that the priest can hear the confessions of members of his congregation.

Do you know

◇ why a cathedral is so called?
◇ what is the focal point in Anglican churches and how this is different from Nonconformist churches?
◇ what the atmosphere in many churches makes those who worship there feel?

Words to remember

Altar   The 'holy table' where the service of Holy Communion takes place.

Cathedral   This comes from Latin word meaning 'throne of a bishop' and is the most important church in an area.

Confessional   A wooden cubicle which separates a person who is confessing their sins from the priest.

Eucharist   This means 'thanksgiving' and is another name for Holy Communion, a service celebrating Jesus's death and Resurrection.

Font   The stone receptacle that holds the water for baptising babies.

Pulpit   The raised platform in a church from which the sermon is delivered.

Things to do

1 In your own words, explain what each of the following is in not more than two sentences:
a   the altar
b   the font
c   the pulpit
d   stained-glass windows
e   the confessional.
If possible, visit a local church. Draw two of these things and find out as much as you can about their history. Is there any interesting feature in the church that has not been mentioned? If so, find out as much as you can about it.

2 Imagine that you are an active member of your local church, and you and your family sometimes take part in different services. Find out, and explain, what you might be likely to do at each of the following:
a   the altar
b   the lectern
c   the font
d   the choir-stalls
e   the pulpit
f   the pews.

How do Christians worship?

Religious worship gives people a practical way to express how they feel about God. As Christian belief centres around Jesus Christ, so he is prominent in all worship. This is clearly seen in the service of Holy Communion which is the most important act of worship in most Churches. You can find out more about this service on pages 56–7.

A A service in an Orthodox church. Orthodox believers like to worship God through the use of ceremony and ritual. How do you think this helps them?

Acts of worship

A Christian act of worship does not have to take place in a church. While Christians still prefer to join together for their worship in a church building, in recent years it has become more popular for them to worship together in 'house-churches'. As their name suggests, these are churches that began by people meeting in each other's houses. Some, however, have grown too large for this and they now have to meet elsewhere.

Whatever the church there are common ingredients to most acts of worship, such as the singing of hymns, the reading of the Bible, praying and listening to a sermon. Through these different means, the Christian believer is seeking forgiveness for past sins and is also looking to God for help to live a better life in the future.

Patterns of worship

The need to worship is felt by all Christians yet the form that this takes varies a great deal from Church to Church:

◆ The older Christian denominations tend to follow a set pattern of worship taken from their own prayer book. For example, in the Church of England, congregations follow either services from the **Book of Common Prayer**, written in 1662, or the much more modern **Alternative Service Book**. Roman Catholics have their own prayer book called the **Missal**.

◆ The Free Churches, such as the Methodist and the Baptist Churches, do not have a prayer book but prefer their minister to lead their worship. In the Salvation Army citadel, a band usually leads the hymns (see picture C).

B
Quakers prefer silence in their services. Why do you think some Christians want to be silent when they are worshipping God?

C
The Salvation Army is rather different from other Christian denominations. What are two differences that you notice from this photograph?

◆ Some smaller Churches do not have a minister or recognised leader to direct their worship. These groups, such as the Quakers, depend on someone in the congregation being 'led by the Spirit' to take the lead. Often in a Quaker meeting most of the time is taken up with private, silent prayer and reflection (see picture B).

Words to remember

Alternative Service Book The prayer book now used in most Church of England churches, first published in 1980.

Book of Common Prayer Drawn up in 1662, this prayer book includes services of the Church of England.

Missal The prayer book which sets out the services of the Roman Catholic Church.

Do you know

◇ what the most important service of worship is in the majority of Churches?
◇ what the *Book of Common Prayer*, the *Alternative Service Book* and the *Missal* are?
◇ which activities make up most acts of worship?

Things to do

1 Look carefully at pictures A, B and C. Describe what you think is going on in each photograph.

2 Give the right word for each of these definitions:
a A group of people who have come together to worship God in a church (a c_____).
b The practical way in which people express what they feel about God (w_____).
c The building in which the Salvation Army members meet to worship (a c_____).
d The part of the service in which a minister might explain a part of the Bible to the people (s_____).

3 In this chapter you have read of several reasons why Christians want to come together to worship God. What are they?

What is Holy Communion?

The most important service in most Churches is the special meal in which Christians celebrate their belief that Jesus died for their sins and rose from the dead (Resurrection). At this service Christians come together to share bread and wine just as Jesus taught his disciples to do in the last meal he had with them. You can read Paul's description of this meal, often called the Last Supper, in the information box.

Different names

Some Christian Churches, for example, the Quakers and the Salvation Army, do not celebrate Holy Communion. In fact, they do not celebrate any of the **sacraments**. Other Churches have their own names, and meaning, for this most important act of worship:

◆ Roman Catholics call the service the **Mass**. They strongly believe that during the most holy part, the bread and wine turn into the actual body and blood of Jesus. This is called **transubstantiation**. Catholics believe that the sacrifice of Jesus for their sins takes place each time the Mass is celebrated.

◆ Anglicans call their celebration the Eucharist or Holy Communion. Some Anglicans hold a belief about the Eucharist being the actual body and blood of Jesus, which is similar to that of Roman Catholics. These people are called **High Anglicans**. Others are much closer to the Nonconformists in their beliefs. For most Anglicans, the bread and wine are a reminder of the last meal that Jesus ate with his disciples.

◆ Nonconformists prefer to call their celebration the **Lord's Supper** or the **Breaking of Bread**. To them the bread and the wine are simply symbols which help them to think

A
These worshippers are receiving the bread and wine during a Roman Catholic Mass. What do worshippers believe happen to them?

Jesus's last supper

In this description Paul explains why Christmas celebrate Holy Communion:

'For I received from the Lord what I also passed on to you: The Lord Jesus, on the night he was betrayed, took bread, and when he had given thanks, he broke it and said, "This is my body, which is for you; do this in remembrance of me". In the same way, after supper he took the cup, saying, "This cup is the new covenant [agreement] in my blood; do this, whenever you drink it, in remembrance of me."'

(1 Corinthians 11.23–5)

◇ What did Jesus tell his disciples after he had broken the bread and what do you think he meant by what he said?
◇ What did Jesus say to his disciples as he gave them the wine and what did he mean by it?

i

about the death and Resurrection of Jesus, and what these two events mean to them personally. It also expresses the bond of the church community.

Words to remember

Breaking of Bread A term used by Nonconformists because, at the Last Supper, Jesus 'broke bread' with his disciples.

High Anglican A member of the Anglican Church whose beliefs and ways of worshipping are similar to a Roman Catholic's.

Lord's Supper This is how Paul described Holy Communion and the title is still used by many Nonconformists.

Mass The Roman Catholic name for the service of Holy Communion. It comes from the last words of the old Latin service – 'Ite missa est' – meaning 'Go, it is finished'.

Sacrament An outward, visible sign of an inward, spiritual blessing obtained through a church service like Holy Communion or baptism.

Transubstantiation The Roman Catholic belief that the bread and wine become the actual body and blood of Christ during the Mass.

B

In their service of Breaking Bread, Baptists are served in their seats with the bread and individual cups of wine. They then all drink together. This has a symbolic meaning. Can you work out what it is?

Do you know

◇ what a sacrament is?
◇ which events in the life of Jesus are recalled by Christians at Holy Communion?
◇ why Christians break bread and drink wine during Holy Communion?

Things to do

1 The *Alternative Service Book* of the Church of England gives this prayer to be used just before the bread and the wine are taken at Holy Communion:

'Accept our praises, heavenly Father, through our Son, Jesus Christ, and as we follow his example and obey his command grant that by the power of your Holy Spirit these gifts of bread and wine may be to us his body and blood.'

How are Christians following Jesus's example and obeying his command by taking part in Holy Communion?

2 In this extract a young Christian is describing why the service of Holy Communion is so important to her:

'In our church when we celebrate Holy Communion we are all remembering that the Lord Jesus Christ died, was buried and rose again from the dead three days later. To me the most important part is the belief that he rose again. This means that one day he will return to this earth again. Every time we celebrate Holy Communion we are being reminded of this fact.'

a Which three events does this young Christian remember every time that she celebrates Holy Communion?
b What does she consider to be the most important part of Holy Communion?
c What does she say that every Christian is looking forward to when they celebrate Holy Communion?

Who are the Church leaders?

Not all Christian Churches have ministers or priests who are professional, full-time leaders. There are those, like the Quakers, who draw their leaders from among the people in the congregation. This allows everyone to use their own special gifts in the service of others and God. Other Churches also make a great use of members of the congregation, or lay people, but certain services – particularly the Eucharist – are taken only by those who have been ordained as priests. This happens in the Anglican, Roman Catholic, Orthodox and Methodist Churches amongst others.

Priests and bishops

After training, a priest is **ordained** to the priesthood. Roman Catholic priests take a vow of **celibacy**, promising not to have sexual relationships and to remain unmarried. No other Church makes this demand on their priests.

The Roman Catholic, Anglican and Orthodox Churches are led by **bishops**. These are senior priests who have responsibility for the churches in their area called

a diocese. Above the bishops in the Roman Catholic Church is the Pope whilst the head of the Anglican Church is the **Archbishop of Canterbury** (see pages 14–15). Below the bishops are the priests who carry out their work in local areas known as parishes. Usually they have more than one church to look after. They are often helped in their work by **deacons** who are able to conduct most services except Holy Communion.

Women priests

There are no women priests in the Roman Catholic and Orthodox Churches – nor do they seem likely in the foreseeable future. Some denominations, though, have ordained women for a long time – including some Anglican, Methodist and Baptist Churches. A long debate in the Church of England finally led to women being ordained for the first time in 1994. In some parts of the Anglican Church women have now been appointed as bishops.

A
This is a Church of England bishop. What do you notice about him from this picture?

Words to remember

Archbishop of Canterbury The leader of the Anglican Church throughout the world, who lives in Lambeth Palace in London. The first Archbishop of Canterbury was Augustine.

Bishop In some Churches, a senior priest who carries responsibility for the churches in an area (called a diocese).

Celibacy The rule in the Roman Catholic Church that priests should not have any sexual relationships or get married.

Deacon An ordained person who can lead some services in the Roman Catholic and Anglican Churches.

Ordination The ceremony by which a person becomes a priest. The bishop lays his hands upon the head of the person to symbolise the Holy Spirit entering them.

Do you know

◇ what ordination is?
◇ who is the head of the Roman Catholic and the Anglican Churches?
◇ which Churches accept women priests and which do not?

B

What do you think are the main tasks which a priest, male or female, should carry out in today's world?

Things to do

1 Answer each of these questions in your own words using the information you are given in this chapter:

a Can you name one branch of the Christian Church which does not have ministers or priests?

b What does it mean when a Roman Catholic priest takes a vow of celibacy?

c What is a deacon?

d What is the name of an area for which a priest is responsible?

e For what is a bishop responsible?

2 The *Book of Common Prayer* includes these words which are spoken by a bishop to a priest who is being ordained:

'A priest is called by God to work with the bishop and with his fellow-priests, as servant and shepherd among the people to whom he is sent. He is to proclaim the word of the Lord, to call his hearers to repentance, and in Christ's name to absolve and to declare the forgiveness of sins. He is to baptise... He is to preside at the celebration of Holy Communion... He is to lead his people in prayer and worship...He is to minister to the sick and prepare the dying for death.'

a Which two words are used here to describe the way that the priest should work among the people? What do you think they mean?

b This passage sets out a list of tasks for the priest. What are they?

Who were the Jewish prophets?

In early Jewish history, a prophet was a man or a woman sent to deliver God's message. Sometimes they would look into the future but, more usually, they passed judgement on the way that the people were living. Probably the first and the greatest of the prophets was Moses. His sister, Miriam, was a prophetess, as was another woman called Deborah.

A
What kind of things might this prophetess be telling the people?

The prophets

The later prophets were to play a very important part in Jewish history. They were mainly teachers of the way people should behave. There was Amos, a herdsman, who suddenly appeared in the market-place and started to preach the judgement of God to the people. Another prophet, Hosea, used his own life story to illustrate how loving and forgiving God is. His wife had been unfaithful to him and he told the Israelites that they, too, had been unfaithful to God by worshipping other gods. However, just as he had taken his wife back, so God would always welcome people who were sorry that they had turned from him.

Then followed a whole line of prophets who told the Jews that God would surely judge and punish them. Isaiah said that God was holy while the nation of Israel was full of hypocrites (two-faced people). They kept all the religious laws but did not look after the poor and the helpless. This message was not popular with the people. One prophet, Jeremiah, was branded a traitor and thrown into prison. He told the people that unless they changed their ways, they would be destroyed.

Jeremiah was not the last of God's messengers to suffer. Daniel was thrown into a lion's den because he refused to stop praying to God when the king told him to do so. Like Jeremiah, though, Daniel survived because God was with him. So, too, did Jonah who was swallowed by a great fish because he refused to preach God's word to the people of Nineveh.

The prophets in the scriptures

Although most of the prophets lived almost 3,000 years ago, they are not forgotten by Jews today. The Jewish scriptures are divided into three sections and after the Torah, the Nevi'im or the Books of the Prophets are the most sacred part. They are divided into two groups:

- The Major Prophets: Isaiah, Jeremiah and Ezekiel
- The Minor Prophets: Daniel, Hosea, Joel, Amos, Obadiah, Jonah, Micah, Nahum, Habakkuk, Zephaniah, Haggai, Zechariah and Malachi.

During services in the synagogue passages from the Books of the Prophets are read after the Torah.

Do you know

◇ what a prophet is?
◇ who was believed to have been the first Jewish prophet?
◇ how Jews keep the message of the prophets alive today?

Why do you think that stories like that of Daniel in the lion's den are still thought to be important by Jews?

Things to do

1 Here is a crossword with the clues filled in. Copy it out. Under your copy, write down one-sentence clues for each of the answers.

2 Unscramble the words in brackets and then copy out the complete sentences into your book:

a Men who spoke on behalf of God to the Jewish people were called (THPOSERP).

b The first Jewish prophet was probably (ESMOS).

c The prophet who likened Israel to his own unfaithful wife was (SOEHA).

d (BREADHO) was a prophetess.

e (RJIAEMEH) was a prophet who was put into prison.

3 Imagine that a prophet, like one of those you have read about, were to visit your country today.

a What kind of things do you think he would have to say?

b Are there any things that he would be happy about?

c What do you think he would be unhappy about?

Illustrate your answer with cuttings from newspapers and magazine articles. Extend this into a wall display of the things which concerned the prophets of old and things which concern people today.

Who were the saints?

A **saint** is a person in the Christian religion who has shown outstanding love for God and holiness during his or her life. Often, although not always, the saint is also a **martyr**: someone who was put to death for their religious beliefs. Sometimes **miracles** are linked with the place where a saint is buried.

The first saints

The first recorded Christian martyr and saint was **Stephen** whose death by stoning is recorded in the Acts of the Apostles. Some years later both Peter and Paul died violently. Although little is known about the actual circumstances of their death, it is thought that it was at the hands of the Roman Emperor, Nero, in 64 CE.

St Polycarp

In the years that followed the deaths of Peter and Paul, most of the original disciples of Jesus were martyred. Then, in 155 CE, the Christian leader, Polycarp, was slaughtered. After his death his bones were collected together by his followers and said to be:

'more precious than jewels of great price.'

They were buried in a safe place but were dug up again when his followers met to commemorate his death. The day of death of a martyr was always considered to be very important because it was believed to be the person's birthday in heaven – the day on which they were reunited with Christ through their death.

Relics

It soon became the custom to bury the bones of a martyr under the altar in a church. This was thought to be the most appropriate place for a servant of Christ to end their days. At the same time the bones, or **relics**, of the saint were thought to have particular healing properties. These places then became shrines – holy places because of their connection with a particular saint.

A

Can you work out anything about this saint from this stained-glass window?

Thousands of people travelled from shrine to shrine as pilgrims hoping to be cured of many different illnesses. Relics were also believed to protect the church that housed them. In the Middle Ages churches often competed against each other to own the most valuable relics.

Nowadays in Britain many of the most popular saints have been largely forgotten. Others, however, still live on in the names of many Anglican and Roman Catholic churches.

Words to remember

Martyr A man or woman who has been put to death because of their Christian beliefs.

Miracle An extraordinary event without a natural explanation.

Relic The bone of a saint or some object associated with them, which is believed to have miraculous healing powers.

Saint A Christian man or woman thought to have lived a particularly holy life. Miracles were often associated with them.

Stephen The first Christian saint to be put to death (martyred). He died after preaching a sermon in Jerusalem declaring his belief that Jesus had risen from the dead.

Do you know

◇ what a saint is?
◇ what a martyr is?
◇ what relics were and why they were thought to be so important?

Things to do

1 Copy out these sentences and fill in the blanks from the words below:

a A _____ is someone who has laid down his or her life for their religious beliefs.

b After the death of a saint, miracles were often associated with their _____.

c Both St _____ and St _____ are believed to have died at the hands of the Roman Emperor _____.

d The bones of St _____ were said to have been 'more precious than jewels of great price.'

e In the Middle Ages the custom was to bury the bones of a saint under the _____ of a church.

Polycarp • altar • Nero • Paul • martyr • relics • Peter

2 Shortly before he was martyred, St Polycarp was given the opportunity of giving up the Christian faith. He is said to have replied:

'For eighty-six years I have been his [Christ's] servant and he has never done me wrong; how can I blaspheme my king who saved me?'

What do you think Polycarp meant when he said this?

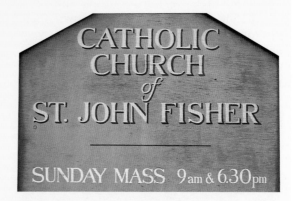

3 This church is dedicated to Saint John Fisher. Find out which saint your local church is dedicated to. Discover as much as you can about it and write up the notes in your book.

4 An ancient writer described the death of Polycarp in the following way:

'When the crowd at the games in the amphitheatre was told that Polycarp had confessed that he was a Christian, they shouted first for the lions and then for him to be burnt at the stake. He was bound; an official killed him with his sword; his body was then burnt.'

Imagine that you are Polycarp. Write an account of the last few minutes of your life and the thoughts that are going through your mind at this time.

Who are monks and nuns?

Soon after the Christian Church began, many men and women wanted to cut themselves off from life in the world and give themselves totally to God. Like Jesus before them, they went into a desert area to pray. Many monks and **hermits** went to Mount Athos in Greece and before long a great number of monasteries had been built in the area. About twenty monasteries remain there, housing thousands of Orthodox monks.

Vows

St Benedict (480–547), who formed the **Benedictine** order of monks, laid down a set of rules for those who joined the community. These became known as 'The Rule' and each monk and **nun** still has to promise to keep these vows or promises today:

♦ To live in total poverty with no earthly possessions. Anything that a person brings with them when they join becomes the property of the monastery or **convent**.

♦ To abstain from all sexual relationships. For nuns this takes the form of being 'married' to God. The wearing of a ring is a symbol of this.

♦ To live in total obedience to the will of the community. In a convent, the authority is the **Mother Superior** and in a monastery, the abbot. The leaders are chosen by the nuns and monks for their holy lives.

A life of prayer

Ever since the first monasteries and convents were built a great emphasis has been placed upon the people in them praying together. By

The number of people entering convents and monasteries has gone down rapidly in recent years. Can you think of two reasons for this?

A

tradition, there are seven times during the day for these prayers or 'offices', although some modern communities reduce this number. They are:

◆ Morning prayers: Lauds (very early morning)
◆ The first hours: Prime (6 a.m.)
◆ The third hour: Terce (9 a.m.)
◆ The sixth hour: Sext (midday)
◆ The ninth hour: None (3 p.m.)
◆ Evening: Vespers (early evening)
◆ Final night prayer: Compline (late evening).

Although most members in a religious community now have work outside the convent or monastery, their lives are still based on prayer. A few communities remain 'enclosed' with little or no contact with the outside world.

Words to remember

Benedictine Based on the teaching of St Benedict, this is one of four well-known Roman Catholic monastic orders.

Convent The place in which nuns live.

Hermit Someone who lives completely on their own. The early Christian hermits lived in the desert and spent time reading the scriptures and praying.

Mother Superior The leader of a community of nuns.

Nun A female member of a religious community who lives in a convent.

St Benedict (480–547) The founder of the first community of monks, who laid down the famous rule of poverty, chastity and obedience, which monks and nuns follow to this day.

Do you know

◇ where thousands of monks set up a cluster of monasteries in Greece?
◇ what the Rule of St Benedict is?
◇ which times of the day are set aside for prayer in a traditional monastery or convent?

B

Why do you think that men and women, over the centuries, have wanted to live in religious communities?

Things to do

1 There are four religious orders in the Roman Catholic Church: the Benedictines, the Franciscans, the Dominicans and the Jesuits. Find out seven pieces of information about one of these.

2 Why do you think that St Benedict insisted on the three rules of poverty, chastity and obedience for his monks? Why do you think they were necessary if people were to live happily with one another?

3 Why do you think that monks and nuns have always put prayer at the very centre of their lives?

4 Do you have a monastery or a convent nearby? If so, try to arrange for a monk or a nun to visit your class to answer questions. Make a list of the questions. You might like to find out, for instance:
a Why the person entered the convent or monastery.
b What life is really like in the convent or monastery.
c Why the person thinks it is important to keep the three vows.

Who were the Sikh Gurus?

In Sikhism there have been ten Gurus, or spiritual teachers, and they are all given great respect. The first was **Guru Nanak** (1469–1539) and he laid down the teachings of the Sikh religion. The last of them was **Guru Gobind Singh** (1666–1708), who told the people that they could not expect God to send them any more human Gurus. From then on they must look to the holy book, the Guru Granth Sahib, to guide and teach them.

The Gurus

Guru Nanak died in 1539 and he chose one of his followers, Lehna (Angad), to succeed him. He made the Punjabi language known to the people so that they could sing the many hymns of Guru Nanak. When Guru Amar Das became leader, he insisted that every Sikh place of worship should have a kitchen (called a langar). Here the rich and the poor could sit down with each other and eat a meal. This has been a feature of every gurdwara ever since (see page 49.)

It was Guru Ram Das who founded the holy city of **Amritsar** in 1577 CE which has become a place of pilgrimage for all Sikhs. It was left to the next Guru, however, to build the Golden Temple there and also to compile the holy book, the Guru Granth Sahib, for everyone to read. Guru Arjan was also the first Sikh martyr. Burning sand was poured over his body by Turkish Muslims before he was made to sit in very hot water and roast to death. The sixth Guru, Guru Har Gobind, encouraged Sikhs to be prepared to die for their faith if necessary. Guru Har Rai and Guru Har Krishan were able to lead peaceful lives but the ninth Guru, Guru Tegh Bahadur, was beheaded by a Muslim emperor of India for insisting that all Sikhs had a right to worship God in their own way.

A
Can you write down five things about Guru Nanak?

The Khalsa

During the time of Guru Gobind Singh, the tenth and last Guru, Sikhs underwent a severe persecution. In 1699 Guru Gobind Singh called them all together in Anandpur. With a drawn sword he asked them:

'Is there anyone who will give up his head to prove his faith in me?'

One man volunteered and went into the tent with Guru Gobind Singh. There was a thud and blood poured out from under the tent flap. This happened four more times with other volunteers but then all five men came out of the tent. They had passed their toughest test and were the first members of the Sikh brotherhood of the **Khalsa** (the pure ones). The Khalsa remains a very important part of Sikhism today.

Words to remember

Amritsar The Sikh holy city in the Punjab region of northern India. It was founded in 1577 CE by the fourth Guru; a place of pilgrimage for all Sikhs.

Guru Gobind Singh The tenth and last human Guru who began the Khalsa brotherhood. His birthday in January is kept as a festival by Sikhs.

Guru Nanak The first Sikh Guru and founder of Sikhism.

Khalsa The Sikh brotherhood (although women can also join) founded by Guru Gobind Singh in 1699. Every new member must pass through an initiation ceremony.

Do you know

◇ who was the first Sikh Guru and why he was particularly important?
◇ who built Amritsar and who began the work of building the Golden Temple there?
◇ which Sikh Guru was responsible for starting the Khalsa?

Things to do

1 This painting shows Guru Gobind Singh, the last human Guru. Why is he important in Sikhism?

2 Imagine that you were one of the five men who volunteered to enter the tent with Guru Gobind Singh.
  a Describe how you might have felt as you made up your mind and went towards it.
  b Imagine that you were a relative of one of these men. Describe your feelings as you heard the thud and saw the blood flowing from under the tent flap.
  c Describe what you felt as the men came walking out of the tent with Guru Gobind Singh.
  d Why do you think that Guru Gobind Singh carried out this test?
  e What was he trying to find out about the men?

Who are Buddhist monks?

The purpose of Buddhism is to help people in their spiritual journey towards **Nirvana**. The order or community of Buddhist monks (the **Sangha**) has always been important in Therevada Buddhism because the simplicity of the monastic life makes the pilgrimage towards Nirvana easier.

Being a monk

Children can become novice monks at the age of seven. They will not be fully ordained as **bhikkus** until they reach the age of twenty and they can leave the monastery at any time. It is believed that they will benefit spiritually even if they only stay for a few weeks or months. In some Buddhist traditions, girls can enter a monastery and they are called bhikkunis.

Monks get up before sunrise and meditate before sweeping the monastery and tending the garden. Then they set off in a line from the monastery to collect their food from local Buddhist householders. The gifts that people give are called **alms**. The monks do not need to beg because Buddhists want to give alms willingly. Buddhism teaches that it is far more important to give than to receive. It is not only part of a Buddhist's duty, but also helps them in their attempt to reach Nirvana.

The monks eat their main meal before noon and after this they fast until the next morning. They may drink water or tea during this time as long as it does not contain milk or sugar. They study and pray, receive friends and sometimes they give people advice. The monks also go out to schools or colleges to speak about Buddhism. They might visit those who are ill in hospital, or in prison. In the early evening the monks often teach people who have come to the **vihara**. The last part of the day is devoted to study and meditation.

Buddhist rules for living

The Five Precepts:

◆ Not to harm any living creature
◆ Not to take something from someone which has not been given
◆ Not to take part in any improper sexual activity
◆ Not to use any improper speech
◆ Not to drink any alcohol or misuse drugs.

Five additional rules for monks:

◆ Not to eat anything after midday
◆ Not to listen to music or dance
◆ Not to use perfumery or jewellery
◆ Not to sleep on a soft bed
◆ Not to accept gifts of money.

Take a close look at these ten rules. Can you think of reasons why Buddhist monks are expected to keep all of them?

A
Why are Buddhists glad to give food freely to the monks?

Living simply

Most Buddhist monks live on their own in a small hut within the monastery. Their rooms are very simple with just a bed and a small table or stool in them. They are expected to sit on the floor. Some rooms also have a small shrine. All that each monk possesses are:

◆ two robes and thread to repair them when they wear out
◆ a razor since most monks keep their heads shaven
◆ a bowl in which people place their gifts and a cup for food and drink
◆ a special strainer to remove any insects from the drinking water. The Buddha taught his followers that they must not kill any living thing – even by accident.

All Buddhists are expected to follow the **Five Precepts** which are a guide for Buddhist living. Monks and nuns are expected to keep five additional rules. All these are given in the information box.

B

Can you find out what meditation is and why it is very important in many religions?

Do you know

◇ what the Sangha is and why it is very important in Buddhism?
◇ how Buddhist monks and nuns are expected to spend their time?
◇ what the Five Precepts are and what additional rules Buddhist monks are expected to keep?

Words to remember

Alms   Gifts which are freely given.

Bhikku   A Buddhist monk. It comes from the word meaning 'beggar' and emphasises the poverty of those who enter Sangha.

Five Precepts   The rules which every Buddhist is expected to keep.

Nirvana   The state of bliss or perfect peace, reached after the struggles of life.

Sangha   The community of monks and nuns founded by the Buddha. Each Buddhist says each day 'I go to the Sangha for refuge'.

Vihara   The term used for the hall in a Buddhist place of worship.

Things to do

1 Monks have very few possessions. Those that they do have include robes, a sun umbrella, thread, a razor and an alms bowl. Why do you think that each of these is very important to a Buddhist monk?

2 Can you think of three reasons why Buddhist parents might want their sons to spend some time in a Buddhist monastery?

3 Some people who are not monks choose to follow the five extra rules as well as the Five Precepts.
   a Why do you think they want to do this?
   b Do you think that following these rules as well as the Five Precepts might make a person's life happier? Can you explain your answer?

4 Find out as much as you can about the life of a Buddhist monk.

Why are symbols used in religious worship?

Symbols are a very important part of worship. Religious people believe that God is so great that he cannot be known. Human language is totally inadequate to describe him. What he is can be partly understood, and experienced, through symbols.

Christian symbols

To Christians God is an all-powerful, invisible and loving Spirit. As such he is totally beyond all human experience. This gap can never be bridged unless links can be found between God and human beings. One useful link for Christians is to call God their 'Father'. The prayer that Jesus taught his disciples to show them how to pray began with the words:

'Our Father, who is in heaven...'

What do Christians mean when they refer to God as their 'Father'? They do not mean that God has 'fathered' them in the same way as their human father. What they are really saying is that God acts towards them as a good father treats his children – firmly with discipline and yet lovingly and tenderly. In this way the symbol – the fatherhood of God – points the worshipper in the direction in which important truths about God can be found. This is the idea behind every religious symbol – to help believers understand more about their faith.

Statues as symbols

A statue or likeness of God is a symbol that is banned in certain religions. The followers of some faiths believe that it is totally wrong to represent God in any human form. For others,

Christians have always found the cross to be a very powerful symbol. What do you think it reminds them of?

70

How do Hindus use murtis like this to worship God?

the statue helps them to focus their hearts and minds on him. As Hindus point out, the murtis in their religion are no more than symbols of their gods. They do not believe that they are gods nor do they worship them. They worship the reality represented by the image.

Most religious buildings are full of symbols; for example, the crescent on a Muslim mosque or the seven-branched candlestick in a Jewish synagogue. Even the flag flying over a Sikh gurdwara is, in itself, a symbol. All religious symbols remind the worshipper that God is over and beyond everything in life yet can be known by those who worship him.

Do you know

◇ why symbols are a great help to some religious worshippers?
◇ one very important Christian symbol which helps worshippers to think about God?
◇ a common Hindu symbol?

Things to do

1 This picture shows the badge of one of the Christian Churches. It contains more than one symbol. Can you find out:
  a which Church uses this as its symbol?
  b the meaning of the different symbols on the badge?

2 Christians, Jews, Muslims and Sikhs are strictly forbidden to make any statues to represent God. For Christians and Jews this is based on one of the Ten Commandments:

> 'You shall not make for yourself an idol in the form of anything in heaven above or on the earth beneath or in the waters below. You shall not bow down to them or worship them; for I, the Lord your God, am a jealous God, punishing the children for the sin of the fathers to the third and fourth generation of those who hate me, but showing love to a thousand generations of those who love me and keep my commandments.'

(Exodus 20.4–6)

  a In this quotation what reason does God give for not allowing any statues or idols?
  b What is demanded from those who want the love of God?
  c Do you think that a statue could help people to worship God? Is there a danger in this?

What are the Christian symbols?

Christians have always found symbols to be very helpful. Hiding from terrible persecution in the Roman Empire, for example, the early Christians drew symbols on the walls of the catacombs beneath Rome. When other Christians saw them, they were encouraged to know that there were friends nearby. Their enemies, on the other hand, could not understand what the symbols meant.

One of the most popular signs at that time was the fish. It was used because each letter of the Greek word for fish (icthus) stood for the phrase:

I – Jesus
C – Christ
TH – God
U – Son of
S – Saviour

The beliefs of early Christians were summed up in the words 'Jesus Christ, Son of God and Saviour'. Many modern Christians have revived this by fixing the symbol of the fish to the back of their cars.

Symbols in worship

Christian worship is full of symbols. At the heart of the Eucharist, the most important Christian service, stand the symbols of bread and wine (see picture A). In the service of **baptism**, when people become members of the Christian Church, the symbol of water is used to teach about spiritual washing and new life. At the serious and joyful season of **Easter** many symbols help the worshipper to think about the death and Resurrection of Jesus. One of these, the Paschal candle, is lit in many churches to symbolise Christians going from darkness to light because of the Resurrection. When a bishop lays his hands upon the heads of those being confirmed as Christians, it is a sign of the Holy Spirit coming to them, just as he did to the disciples at Pentecost (see page 6). The Holy Spirit is usually symbolised as a dove.

The symbol of the cross

The most important and powerful Christian symbol of all is the cross, found both inside and outside almost all churches. It highlights the death of Jesus for the sins of the whole world. Sometimes there is a figure of Jesus on the cross – this is called a **crucifix**. Christians often wear small crosses around their necks as a symbol of their membership of the Church.

Some Christians, mainly High Anglicans and Roman Catholics, touch their forehead, chest and shoulders with their hand in the sign of the cross during certain acts of worship. Some people also **genuflect** in front of the altar on entering a church and make the sign of the cross. At the end of the service, the priest often blesses the congregation, making the sign of the cross above the heads of the people as he does so (see picture B).

A Can you remember what the bread and wine symbolise in the service of Holy Communion?

B
What is this priest doing, and why?

Words to remember

Baptism The service in which a person becomes a member of the Christian Church. Most people are baptised as babies, but in the Baptist Church adults only are baptised.

Crucifix A cross with the figure of Christ on it.

Easter The Christian festival which celebrates the death and the Resurrection of Jesus.

Genuflect To kneel briefly on the right knee with the body straight. Some Christians do this in front of the altar in church as a mark of respect.

Do you know ?

◇ which symbol gave Christians great courage while suffering persecution from the Romans? What did it symbolise?
◇ in which Christian celebrations symbols play an important part?
◇ what is the central Christian symbol?

Things to do

1 The following text was found on the tombstone of an early Christian. It suggests the thoughts of a man who was in danger of being persecuted:

'My name is Avircius, a disciple of the pure Shepherd, who feeds the flocks of sheep on mountains and plains, who has great and all-seeing eyes. He taught me the faithful Scriptures. To Rome he sent me. Everywhere I met with brethren. With Paul before me I followed, and Faith everywhere led the way and served food everywhere, the Fish from the spring – immense, pure, which the pure virgin caught and gave to her friends to eat for ever, with good wine, giving the cup with the wine.'

The writer here uses several Christian symbols. How many can you find?

2 The symbols on this banner link two great Christian festivals. What are they?

What are the important Jewish symbols?

There are many symbols which play an important part in Jewish life. Jews believe that it is possible to worship God equally well in the home and in the synagogue so religious symbols are found in both these places.

What does the mezuzah symbolise in a Jewish home and why is this person touching it with his fingertips?

Symbols in the home

The Jewish religion provides guidelines for every aspect of life. Most men and women follow a dietary code regarding the food they eat which is laid down in the Torah. These laws are known as **kashrut** and say that Jews can eat only:

◆ animals that chew the cud and have completely parted hooves
◆ birds such as chicken, duck and turkey
◆ fish that have fins and scales.

Food that is permitted is called **kosher**. Kosher food is a symbol of the purity and obedience that God requires of all Jews.

An important symbol in a Jewish home is the **mezuzah** (see picture A). This is a small, hand-written scroll containing part of the Shema, a prayer from the Torah. The scroll is placed in a decorative case and one is attached to most of the doorposts in the home. Some people lightly kiss the fingertips of their right hand and touch the mezuzah as they go in and out of each room. In this way they are showing respect for the Torah and its teaching.

Symbols in the synagogue

Amongst the most important symbols found in a synagogue are the Ark and the **Everlasting Light** that burns above it. The Ark is the holiest part of the synagogue since it houses the scrolls of the Torah, which Jews believe is God's greatest gift to the Jewish people. The Everlasting Light reminds them that God is always with them.

Many synagogues also contain a **Star of David** (picture B). This six-pointed star is made up of two equilateral triangles: one pointing up and the other down. No one is quite sure how it came to be associated with King David but it has been found on Jewish buildings since the twelfth century. Known as the 'magen David', it is the symbol of the State of Israel.

During the Second World War over six million Jews were put to death by the Nazis. Why do you think that the Star of David became a very important symbol to Jews during this time?

Words to remember

Everlasting Light The light that shines all the time above the Ark in the synagogue as a reminder that God is always with the Jews.

Kashrut The Jewish laws governing food.

Kosher This means 'fit'; food that is permitted under Jewish dietary laws.

Mezuzah A small parchment scroll containing part of the Shema. It is placed inside a cover and fixed to most of the door frames in a house.

Star of David The six-pointed star which is a symbol of the State of Israel.

Do you know

◇ what is symbolised by the light shining over the Ark in the synagogue?
◇ what the mezuzah is?
◇ why the dietary laws called 'kashrut' are very important to all Jews?

Things to do

1 Copy this paragraph into your book and fill in the blanks from the words listed below:

The Jewish faith makes extensive use of _____ both in the _____ and in the _____. In the synagogue the _____ _____ above the _____ symbolises the _____ of God with his people. The _____ laws are a very important symbol of obedience to the will of God. The laws governing the food that Jews are allowed to eat are called _____. They are laid down in the _____. Permitted food is called _____ and is a very important symbol in the home.

Torah • Everlasting Light • symbols • synagogue • kashrut • home • kosher • presence • Ark • dietary

2 In a radio programme, 'Worlds of Faith', a Jewish mother explained how every act of her day became 'religious':

'All the daily chores of a woman become, for a Jewish woman, religious acts. For example, shopping, cleaning, cooking; when I go shopping I have to remember our dietary laws and be very careful about the food I select in the market... we elevate everything to God – even, for example, the cleaning; we have to clean before Shabbat [the Sabbath Day] and before the Holy Days [festivals] and that is actually a positive commandment.'

When asked why she keeps all the commandments, she said:

'Just because God commanded it... There are many commandments we don't understand. We can try to find reasons for them but lots of them we simply don't understand.'

a What example does this woman give of turning the everyday things of life into religious acts?
b What is her reason for doing this?

What are the symbols of Islam?

The main symbols of Islam are the crescent moon and a star, found on every mosque. Both of these are very important in the Middle East, where there are many Muslims, as they guide desert people at night. The Prophet Muhammad grew up in a city in which the stars and the moon were worshipped but he attacked this. They were, however, suitable symbols for the new faith since Islam is believed to guide mankind (the star) and light the way of every believer through life (moon).

The dome and the minarets

It is an important belief of Islam that, although the imam may lead the public prayers, each Muslim must come into the presence of God himself. The shape of the mosque is designed to help followers to concentrate their mind on God. As picture A shows, the dome is an important feature of every mosque. It symbolises the heavens and the universe which Allah has created and over which he reigns. The minaret, from which the mu'adhin calls the faithful to prayer, is like a beacon shining in the darkness of the world around.

Minarets also serve as a symbol in another way. There are usually four of them on a mosque and together with the dome they are a reminder of the Five Pillars of Islam. These are the compulsory duties that every Muslim must undertake:

◆ **Shahadah** – the Muslim declaration of faith which is set out in the information box.

◆ **Salah** – every Muslim must pray five times a day in the way taught by the Prophet Muhammad.

◆ **Zakah** – each Muslim must give 1/40 of his savings to help the poor.

◆ **Sawm** – every healthy Muslim must fast (go without food or drink, including water) during the daylight hours of the month of **Ramadan**.

A
What does the minaret and the dome of the mosque symbolise for the Muslim?

The Shahadah

'There is no god except Allah, Muhammad is the Messenger of Allah.'

What are the two most important aspects of Muslim belief which are stressed in the Shahadah?

B
This picture shows a Muslim prostrating, but what is he doing?

◆ **Hajj** – at least once during their lifetime, Muslims must go on the annual pilgrimage to the holy city of Makkah (see page 90).

The place of prostration

In the Qur'an, Muhammad said:

'The whole earth has been made a place of prostration for me.'

As long as he is in a clean place a Muslim can pray anywhere. Together with performing wudu (which must go before any prayers), this underlines the purity that Allah demands from those who worship him. During and at the end of his prayers, a Muslim prostrates himself (kneels down with his forehead touching the floor) in the presence of God (picture B). All of these actions symbolise the submission and obedience which Allah demands of those who seek his forgiveness.

Words to remember

Hajj The annual pilgrimage to Makkah, which every Muslim must make at least once in a lifetime.

Ramadan The ninth month of the Muslim year, kept as a time of fasting when no food or drink are taken during daylight hours.

Salah The strict Muslim duty to pray five times a day in the way taught by Muhammad.

Sawm The practice of fasting during the month of Ramadan.

Shahadah The Muslim statement of belief in Allah and Muhammad, his Prophet.

Zakah The obligation on every Muslim to give 1/40 of his income every year to help the poor.

Do you know ?

◇ why the crescent moon and the star are suitable symbols for Islam?
◇ how the dome and minarets on a mosque remind a Muslim of his duties?
◇ what other symbols are important in Islam?

Things to do

1 The Qur'an describes how Abraham (Ibrahim) turned from worshipping the sun, moon and stars to the worship of Allah:

'Accordingly, We [God] showed Abraham the Kingdom of the heavens and of the earth, that he might be one of sure faith. As night darkened around him he beheld a star and said: "This is my Lord." But when it set, he said, "I cannot love what sets." And when he saw the moon rising he said, "If my Lord does not guide me aright, I shall surely be among the erring." And when he saw the sun rising he said, "This is my Lord, this is greater." But when it also set he said, "O my people I have finished with all your idolatrous things [worshipping things rather than God]. As for me my face is towards the One who created the heaven and the earth, as a man of pure faith. I am not a worshipper of false deities [gods]."'

a Why do you think that Ibrahim, who lived in a desert area, was tempted to worship the stars, moon and sun?
b What was it that persuaded him not to worship them in the end?
c What was there about God which made him greater than the heaven and the earth?

2 A Muslim must wash himself before praying and prostrate himself as he prays. Explain, in your own words, why these actions are important and what they mean.

What are the symbols of Hinduism?

In Hinduism, everything that exists is part of **Brahman**, the Supreme Spirit. Because of this anything can be used to help to focus a Hindu's mind on God during worship. Murtis and other images are not themselves the object of worship. They do, however, point to the Supreme Spirit with whom each Hindu, after many rebirths, hopes to be reunited. When this happens a Hindu's life on earth is complete.

Ganesha

There are thought to be some 330,000,000 Hindu gods. Most families have their own particular one whose murti has a place in the shrine in their home. Each person finds their own murti full of symbolism and this helps them to worship their particular deity. We can see this if we look at just one popular Hindu

god – **Ganesha** – who has the head of an elephant.

a   Ganesha has four hands. In two hands he holds a string of beads, or rosary, and a goad (stick). The rosary is a symbol of Ganesha's control over death whilst the goad is used to make each human being behave. In his other two hands are an axe by which he destroys ignorance and sweets to reward those whose ignorance has been taken away.

b   Around the neck of Ganesha is a snake as a necklace. In many religions the snake is a symbol of evil. Here Ganesha is in perfect control of it and so able to offer men and women the power to conquer evil.

c   The God sits on a mouse. As Ganesha is an elephant this shows his concern for all creatures, great and small.

What does a Hindu believe about everything that exists in the world?

A

This picture shows Hanuman, the monkey-god. Why are murtis an important part of Hindu worship?

d   From Ganesha's mouth comes the most sacred of Hindu words, **aum**. This is made up of three sounds – a, u and m – and represents:

♦ the three Vedas, the ancient Hindu holy books

♦ the three worlds – the Earth, the Atmosphere and Heaven

♦ the three main Hindu gods – Brahma, Vishnu and Shiva.

The word is believed to contain all the secrets of the universe and is spoken before reading the Hindu scriptures, prayer, meditation and any act of worship

Words to remember

Aum   The most sacred Hindu symbol and sound.

Brahman   The supreme soul, the power beyond the universe, from which everything comes, in which it rests and all returns.

Ganesha   A popular deity in Hinduism, the god of wisdom and good fortune.

Do you know

◇ whether Hindus believe in millions of gods or one God?
◇ what a Hindu eventually hopes to achieve?
◇ what symbols are found on the murti of the popular elephant-god, Ganesha?

Things to do

Fit together the phrases below to make a sensible paragraph. Make a rough draft and see if your classmates agree, then copy it into your book.

a   to help the people draw nearer to Brahman
b   although there are many gods in Hinduism
c   in its upward march to God
d   they are all representations of the one all-embracing spirit, Brahman
e   each god is an aid
f   each murti of a god is a symbol
g   to achieve union with Brahman
h   to help the soul

What are the symbols of Sikhism?

Not only is Sikhism a religious faith but it is also a community of believers, a fellowship and a brotherhood. Sikhs can offer up prayers to God at any time but must meet regularly with their fellow believers for communal worship. As the Guru Granth Sahib says:

> 'The highest and the most beneficial deed is the Lord's praise in the holy congregation.'

The gurdwara as a symbol

The gurdwara, the place of worship, is a symbol of the unity which exists between all Sikhs. That unity is also symbolised by the flag that flies over every gurdwara indicating that this is a Sikh place of worship. There are three symbols on the triangular flag:

◆ two kirpans (one of the Five Ks – see opposite)
◆ a circle
◆ the **khanda**.

The central symbols are military because a Sikh sees himself as a holy warrior. In times past he has often been called upon to defend his faith by taking up the sword. Another khanda is placed at the top of the flag-pole to emphasise this.

A Which symbols are found on the Sikh flag, and what do they tell you about the way that a Sikh understands his faith?

B Write down three features of Sikh worship that you notice from this photograph.

The Five Ks

A Sikh, on joining the Khalsa (see page 67), is presented with five symbols. These are called the **Five Ks** (panj kakke). They are all very important symbols worn or carried by Sikhs:

◆ **Kesh** – long hair. Uncut hair is a sign of dedication to God and to the faith.

◆ **Kangha** – the comb. This is needed to keep the hair clean. It is a symbol of the physical and spiritual cleanliness which God requires of all Sikhs.

◆ **Kara** – the steel band worn on the right wrist. It shows that the wearer is faithful to the teachings of the Gurus. The circle of the bracelet is a symbol of eternity and of unity.

◆ **Kachera** – traditional underwear/shorts. This is a sign that the person is always ready to fight for the faith.

◆ **Kirpan** – a short sword. A symbol of the power and freedom which people find in Sikhism. It also shows that a member of the Khalsa is a spiritual warrior.

The holy book

The Guru Granth Sahib, the holy book, is the most precious possession belonging to the Sikhs. It is also the most important symbol of their faith. They do not worship it but they treat it with the greatest possible reverence because of what it symbolises. Whenever it is present that place becomes a gurdwara and God is known to be there.

Do you know

◇ what the gurdwara and the flag flying above it symbolise?
◇ what the Guru Granth Sahib symbolises?
◇ what each of the Five Ks symbolises?

Words to remember

Five Ks The five symbolic items worn or carried by members of the Khalsa.

Kachera Underwear/shorts worn by members of the Khalsa to show that they are ready to fight for their faith.

Kangha The symbolic wooden comb worn by members of the Khalsa.

Kara A steel band worn on the right wrist by members of the Khalsa.

Kesh The long hair worn by members of the Khalsa. It is tied in a special knot and covered by a turban.

Khanda A double-edged sword, used in the Amrit ceremony.

Things to do

1 About the gurdwara which symbolises the unity between Sikhs, the Guru Granth Sahib says:

'Holy congregation is the school of the True Guru. There we learn to love God and appreciate his goodness.'

a Who do you think the 'True Guru' is and why is he called 'True'?
b What is a congregation, and to what does it refer here?
c Why is it called 'holy'?
d Why is the holy congregation called the 'school' of the True Guru?
e In learning to appreciate their unity with each other what two things does a Sikh learn?

2 In picture A you can see a Sikh flag.
a What do all flags symbolise?
b Why do you think that a flag is chosen to let everyone know that a particular building is a gurdwara?

What are the symbols of Buddhism?

The three most important symbols in Buddhism are the wheel, the lotus flower and the Buddha.

The wheel

The wheel is the main symbol for Buddhists. It has eight spokes and is a reminder that the teaching of the Buddha is summed up in the Eightfold Path. This sets out the 'Middle Way', explaining how everyone who wants to reach Nirvana should live. Buddhists should not live a life of luxury, nor should they deprive themselves of so much comfort that they become ill. The Middle Way involves the following:

- right viewpoint
- right thought
- right speech
- right action
- right living
- right effort
- right awareness
- right meditation.

B

How does the Buddhist use the lotus flower as a symbol of the spiritual growth which each person must make?

The lotus flower

The lotus flower is another important symbol. The roots of the lotus grow in muddy water and the petals rise up and open out towards the sun. This symbolises the growth of the Buddhist towards spiritual enlightenment. Just as there are many different colours of the lotus flower so there are many different kinds of people.

The Buddha

Buddha is a title meaning 'the enlightened one'. Although there have been thousands of Buddhas, or spiritual teachers, the statues are always of Siddharta Gautama, the founder of the religion. Although he can be shown in different positions, such as standing up or lying down, he is most likely to be in the 'lotus position' as in picture C. The thumb and first finger of one hand form a circle. This symbolises his first teachings when he gave the laws of life to his followers. A bump on the top of his head shows that he has special gifts. A 'third eye' in the middle of his forehead

A
What is the eight-spoked wheel a reminder to Buddhists of?

What can you remember about the background to the life of Siddharta Gautama Buddha?

symbolises the belief that Buddha can 'see' things that no one else notices. His long ear-lobes indicate that he came from an important family, while his curled hair shows that he was a holy man.

Questions of King Malinda

An old Buddhist book has this to say:

'Just as the lotus, though it is born in the water, and grows up in the water, yet remains undefiled [unspoilt] by the water, just so should the strenuous monk, earnest in effort, remain undefiled.'

The lotus flower remains undefiled by the muddy water. What is the monk to be undefiled by?

Do you know

◇ what teaching of the Buddha is highlighted by the symbol of the wheel?
◇ how the lotus flower teaches a Buddhist about spiritual growth?
◇ which symbols are shown by the Buddha sitting in the lotus position?

Things to do

1 Look carefully at picture C. Explain the meaning of:
   a the bump on the Buddha's head
   b the 'third eye'
   c the long ear-lobes
   d the curly hair.

2 Mandalas are a popular symbol in Buddhism. Find out all that you can about them. Draw a mandala in your book and explain the meaning of the different symbols on it.

Where are the holy places?

A pilgrimage is a journey undertaken by followers of a religion to places that are believed to be particularly holy. Some people go on such a journey because of the deep peace that it can bring. Others use a pilgrimage to express their own deep faith. Many pilgrims travel for the experience of meeting with other believers, while others travel to find healing from disease or illness. In some religions, such as Islam, a solemn obligation is placed on believers to make the journey.

Hindu holy places

There are many holy places in Hinduism and worshippers are likely to make several visits to them during their lifetime. Often the main reason for the journey is to meet their guru or spiritual teacher. Although these holy places can be in the mountains, Hindus have long regarded the rivers of India as being the most holy places of all. This is particularly true of those places where two rivers meet, as at **Varanasi**.

The city of Jerusalem

When the Jewish Temple was still standing in Jerusalem 2,000 years ago, all Jews were expected to visit the city three times a year for the great pilgrimage festivals. The Temple was destroyed in 70 CE but thousands of pilgrims still visit the city each year. Whilst Jerusalem is still sacred to Jews, it is also holy for all Christians and Muslims.

Christian holy places

Although Christians are not under any obligation to make pilgrimages, thousands of them do so. The most popular destination is Palestine, known as the Holy Land, and the places associated with Jesus. Thousands of Christians also travel to places such as Lourdes, in France, and Walsingham, in Norfolk, where the **Virgin Mary** is said to have appeared.

Muslim holy places

As long as they are fit and healthy, Muslims must make the hajj or pilgrimage to the holy city of Makkah at least once in their lifetime. This is one of the Five Pillars of Islam (see page 76). On the pilgrimage they will also visit other places which have played an important part in Muslim history. Those who are unable to go can financially support someone who is making the journey or can pay for someone who has already visited Makkah to make the journey on their behalf.

Do you know

◇ which are the most holy places for Hindus?
◇ which city is holy to three different religions, and what those religions are?
◇ who makes a special journey to Makkah and what the journey is called?

A
Why do you think rivers are considered holy places in Hinduism?

Why do you think every Muslim will gain from making a journey to the places associated with the Prophet Muhammad?

Words to remember

Varanasi A town situated on the banks of the River Ganges, one of the most sacred places in Hinduism. To die there is a great blessing, offering the gateway to eternal life.

Virgin Mary The mother of Jesus Christ, highly honoured by many Christians, especially Roman Catholics.

Things to do

1 Hidden in this word puzzle are five words connected with pilgrimages to holy places. The words read across or down. Find them and explain what each one means.

L	A	M	E	C	T	C	A	G	N
V	A	R	A	N	A	S	I	O	L
T	F	K	I	V	M	W	I	R	H
E	M	L	J	G	P	R	J	G	U
M	L	W	Q	S	L	U	V	H	D
P	A	G	J	M	A	K	K	A	H
L	O	U	R	D	E	S	H	J	Y
E	I	J	N	N	R	C	V	J	I
P	A	M	E	D	Z	V	U	S	T

2 In the Qur'an, all Muslims are told they must go on a pilgrimage to Makkah at some time. Here are the words:

'Exhort all men to make the pilgrimage. They will come on foot, and on the backs of swift camels and from every quarter. Let the pilgrims spruce themselves, make their vows and circle the Ancient House.

Such is Allah's commandment. He that reveres the sacred rites of Allah shall fare better in the sight of the Lord.'

Why do you think that some religions lay a heavy obligation upon a believer to make a pilgrimage whilst others do not?

Why is Jerusalem important?

Jerusalem is very important to three different religions: Christianity, Judaism and Islam. It was here that King David made his capital city and his son, Solomon, put up the first great Temple in 950 BCE. And it was here that Jesus was crucified. The city today has many places that are sacred to Christians, Jews and Muslims.

The Wailing Wall

Solomon's temple was destroyed in 586 BCE and after more than five hundred years a replacement was built by Herod the Great around the time of Jesus. The Romans destroyed it in 70 CE. All that now remains of Herod's majestic building is the Western Wall, known as the **Wailing Wall**. For hundreds of years Jewish pilgrims have prayed here, rocking backwards and forwards reciting their holy Torah (see picture A). By doing this they are expressing their great sorrow that the Jewish people have been scattered throughout the world. They are also praying for God's future blessing on Jews everywhere.

Christians and Jerusalem

For Christians, Jerusalem is a very special city associated, as it is, with the life and death of Jesus of Nazareth. As a Jew, and knowing that death was near, Jesus made his way to the city since he considered it to be the only fit place for a prophet to die. In the courtyard of the Roman governor, Pontius Pilate, he was tried and sentenced to death. In the same city, three days later, his disciples rejoiced at his return from the dead.

Christians visit Jerusalem at any time but most go during the days leading up to the great festival of Easter. On **Good Friday** they follow in the footsteps of Jesus by walking along the **Via Dolorosa**. Some pilgrims carry crosses over their shoulders. They also visit the **Church of the Holy Sepulchre**, built where the tomb of Jesus is believed to have been.

Muslims in Jerusalem

After Makkah and Madinah, Jerusalem is the most holy, and important, city in Islam. The **Dome of the Rock**, a Muslim shrine, commemorates the 'Night Journey' which the Prophet Muhammad made on a winged horse through the seven spheres of heaven to meet with Allah. From Allah's presence Muhammad returned to the earth to preach the message that he had received. It is this message which has persuaded millions of people to become Muslims.

A
What are these Jews doing at the Wailing Wall in Jerusalem?

B

Why is the city of Jerusalem holy to Muslims?

Words to remember

Church of the Holy Sepulchre A church in Jerusalem, built upon the supposed site of the tomb of Jesus.

Dome of the Rock A mosque in Jerusalem, built on the rock from which Muhammad is said to have ascended into heaven.

Good Friday The day on which Christians commemorate the death of Jesus.

Via Dolorosa The street in Jerusalem up which Jesus walked on the way to his crucifixion.

Wailing Wall The only part of Herod's Temple still standing, a place of pilgrimage for Jews.

Do you know

◇ what makes the city of Jerusalem special to Jews, Muslims and Christians?
◇ what the Wailing Wall is?
◇ what the Church of the Holy Sepulchre and the Dome of the Rock are?

Things to do

1 On one occasion St Matthew tells us that Jesus was very upset over the future of the city of Jerusalem. He records Jesus as saying:

'O Jerusalem, Jerusalem, you who kill the prophets and stone those sent to you, how often I have longed to gather your children together, as a hen gathers her chicks under her wings, but you were not willing. Look, your house is left to you desolate.'

(Matthew 23.27–8)

a What do you think Jesus meant when he said that he had often wanted to gather the children of Jerusalem together?
b When was the Temple in Jerusalem left 'desolate'?

2 Visit your library and find out as much as you can about the city of Jerusalem. Try to find pictures of the Wailing Wall, the Church of the Sepulchre and the Dome of the Rock. Write the information up in your books as a short project.

What are the Christian holy places?

The holy places of pilgrimage which Christians have visited for centuries have drawn pilgrims for a variety of reasons:

◆ to give thanks for something that God or the saint is believed to have done for them
◆ to say a special prayer
◆ to seek healing
◆ to express repentence for a wrong-doing and to seek God's forgiveness.

Christian places of pilgrimage can be put into two groups:

◆ those in the Holy Land of Israel where events in the life of Jesus took place. This includes the city of Jerusalem and Bethlehem, the birthplace of Jesus.

◆ those which are associated with saints, where they are buried or are believed to have had visions.

This chapter concentrates on places of pilgrimage connected with the saints, in Britain and overseas.

Pilgrimages in Britain

The most well-known shrine in Britain is at **Walsingham**, in Norfolk. In 1061 the Lady of the Manor, Richeldis de Faverches, had three visions of the Virgin Mary. She was transported to a house in Nazareth and she was told to build an exact replica in Walsingham. It was destroyed in the sixteenth century but rebuilt in 1931. Anglicans and Catholics now visit the shrine and process through the village each year.

Places of pilgrimage overseas

In Europe, there are many places which Christian pilgrims have travelled to in the past – and still do so today. With its many links with the early Christian Church, the city of Rome receives many visitors. During festival times, especially at Easter, Christians gather in St Peter's Square to receive the Pope's blessing. Pilgrims also visit the home of St Francis in Assisi. This thirteenth-century saint is famous for his loving care of birds and animals.

Often pilgrims undertake a journey to seek healing. It was at **Lourdes**, in 1850, that a 14-year-old girl, Bernadette, had 18 visions of the Virgin Mary. A spring of water appeared and then a series of miraculous healings is said to have started. About 1,000,000 people visit Lourdes each year and most of them are sick or handicapped. Even though a very small handful of people have been cured, the majority return with a deep sense of God's peace.

A
Anglicans and Roman Catholics have their separate churches in Walsingham. Why do you think this is so?

Why do you think so many Christians gather to receive the Pope's blessing?

Words to remember

Lourdes A centre of Christian pilgrimage in southern France. The place where Bernadette had a series of visions of the Blessed Virgin Mary. People started to be healed here from 1873 onwards.

Walsingham The most important place of pilgrimage in Britain. The first shrine was built in the eleventh century and was an exact copy of the house of Jesus in Nazareth.

Do you know

◇ why many Christian pilgrims decide to make a pilgrimage to a holy place?
◇ why thousands of pilgrims visit Lourdes each year?
◇ what the link is between the shrines at Lourdes and Walsingham?

Things to do

1 Here are five definitions. What are they referring to?
   a The Christian shrine founded as the result of visions experienced by a 14-year-old girl.
   b The centre of pilgrimage which was the home of a saint who became famous for his care of birds and animals.
   c The country in which Jesus lived and which has many centres of pilgrimage.
   d The square in Rome in which pilgrims gather to receive a blessing from the Pope.
   e The shrine which is based on the house in which Jesus grew up.

2 Copy an outline map of Europe into your book. Using this chapter and your own research put as many places of Christian pilgrimage as you can on the map.

Can you discover what is thought to have happened at one of these places that has made it special to pilgrims?

Note: As well as those places mentioned in this chapter, the following are also important centres of pilgrimage: Canterbury in England; Santiago de Compostello in Spain; Lindisfarne; Iona; Knock in Ireland.

89

What is the hajj?

All healthy Muslims, male and female, must make the hajj, the annual pilgrimage to the holy city of Makkah, at least once during their lifetime. It is one of the Five Pillars of Islam (see page 76). As the Qur'an tells them:

> 'Make the pilgrimage and visit the Sacred House for His sake... Make the pilgrimage in the appointed month.'

The 'appointed month' is the ninth in the Muslim calendar – Ramadan, during which Muslims must fast. Each year about 2,000,000 pilgrims make their way to Makkah from all over the world.

In Makkah

As they reach the outskirts of Makkah, male pilgrims put on two pieces of cloth to symbolise **ihram**, the state of purity entered by those making the hajj. They call out:

> 'We have come in answer to your call, O Lord.'

Once in the city each pilgrim performs the **tawaf** by walking seven times (three times quickly and four times slowly) around the Ka'bah in worship of Allah. (You can see what this cube-like structure looks like in picture B.) Moving in a clockwise direction, and always keeping the Ka'bah on their left-hand side, each pilgrim tries to kiss the **Black Stone** at the base of the Ka'bah. This Stone was believed to have been given by God to Ibrahim (Abraham). It was once white but has turned black because of the sins of the human race.

Outside Makkah

You can see from diagram A the route which pilgrims take once they have left Makkah. It was between Safa and Marwa that Ishma'il's mother ran frantically to and fro looking for water – only to discover that her young son had already been shown a well in the desert by God. To relive this event, each pilgrim must run the 366 metres between the two places seven times.

The following day, after sunrise, the pilgrims set out for Mount Arafat. Some walk and others ride. Once there the pilgrims offer prayers remembering the words of Muhammad that:

> 'the best of prayers is that of the day of Arafat'.

Then, after spending the night in the open, the pilgrims collect 49 stones on their way to Mina. Once there they throw the stones at three concrete pillars. These represent the devil and remind the pilgrim that Ishma'il was tempted by the devil to rebel against his father, Ibrahim. It is believed that Ishma'il drove the devil away by throwing stones at him.

Mount Arafat

Plain of Arafat

Muzdalifah

Mina

Safa and Marwa

The Ka'bah in Makkah

A Copy this diagram into your book and notice what happens at each of the places mentioned.

B
Can you find out why pilgrims walk seven times around the Ka'bah?

Id-ul-Adha

The great festival of **Id-ul-Adha** held at Mina ends the period of hajj. It is celebrated by all Muslims, whether they are on the pilgrimage or not. It commemorates Ibrahim's willingness to sacrifice his first-born son's life to God. Muslims make a sacrifice of an animal, usually a sheep. In this way Muslims everywhere are sharing in the blessings that all those who have taken part in the pilgrimage have enjoyed.

Words to remember

Black Stone   One of the most sacred objects in Islam, set in the south-east corner of the Ka'bah.

Id-ul-Adha   The Festival of Sacrifice, which takes place when pilgrims reach Mina.

Ihram   A state of purity which is symbolised by two cotton cloths that a pilgrim must put on before entering Makkah. One of them is wound around the waist and the other is draped across the left shoulder. Women wear their normal modest dress, with their heads covered but their faces unveiled.

Ka'bah   The sacred shrine in Makkah, set in the courtyard of the mosque. Wherever they are in the world, all Muslims face towards the Ka'bah when they pray.

Tawaf   Walking around the Ka'bah seven times at the start of the hajj pilgrimage, in worship of Allah.

Do you know

◇ who is expected to make the pilgrimage to Makkah?
◇ what pilgrims do in the city of Makkah?
◇ what pilgrims do after they leave Makkah?

Things to do

1 When pilgrims enter Makkah they call out:

> 'We have come in answer to your call, O Lord.'

This sums up the real reason for every Muslim making the pilgrimage. What do you think that reason is?

2 Muslim pilgrims change into the dress of ihram when they reach the outskirts of Makkah:
a What is ihram?
b Why do you think that every pilgrim wears exactly the same clothes?

3 Here are two Muslims speaking after their experience of making a hajj pilgrimage to Makkah:

◆ 'It is every Muslim's ambition to visit the blessed city of Makkah and kiss the Black Stone. For me that was a very beautiful experience. It was also very moving to visit the Prophet's tomb in Madinah later.'

◆ 'Although it is many years since I went on the hajj I can still remember very clearly how I felt when I stood in front of the Ka'bah. Once you are there you feel that you are in paradise and not on earth at all. The actual journey may be hard work but once you are there everything is so worthwhile.'

a What do you think there was about standing in front of Muhammad's tomb that made it such a moving experience for the first speaker?
b What could the second speaker mean when he says his visit to Makkah makes you feel you are in paradise?

What happens at Varanasi?

Rivers play a very important part in the everyday lives of people in India, which is where most Hindus come from. They irrigate surrounding land, making it fertile, as well as providing water for washing, drinking and cooking. In view of this, it is not surprising that rivers are looked upon as 'mother goddesses'. Most of the holy places that Hindus visit regularly are situated on the banks of rivers.

Varanasi

The greatest of all the holy places is the city of **Varanasi** (see picture B). Its sacredness comes from its location – on the banks of the River Ganges where the river meets its smaller tributary, the Varuna. The meeting-place of two rivers is thought by Hindus to be particularly holy.

The holiness of Varanasi is greatly increased by the Hindu belief that the great god **Shiva** (see picture A) lived here. This draws more than 1,000,000 pilgrims to the city each year and there are over 1,000 temples dedicated to Shiva alone. Shiva is the Hindu god of life, death and rebirth. He is the visible form of the power who both creates life and destroys it. As you can see from picture A, he is often shown taking part in a world-shattering dance.

A

The god Shiva is both loved and hated by Hindus. Can you suggest why?

Ghats

Along the three-mile stretch of the Ganges in Varanasi there are steps called **ghats** from which Hindu pilgrims are able to bathe in the holy waters of the river. This cleanses the body after a long journey but also, more importantly, cleanses the soul from all evil.

The cremation (burning) of dead bodies is carried out on the steps before the ashes and sacred marigold leaves are placed on the waters. It is the dearest wish of every Hindu to die in Varanasi and to have their ashes scattered on the waters of the Ganges. They believe that this will guarantee that their soul will pass straight to Brahman without needing to be reborn again. This is extremely important in a religion which believes strongly in **reincarnation**.

Do you know

◇ where the city of Varanasi is situated and what makes its position so important?
◇ which god is worshipped in Varanasi in particular?
◇ what the Hindu pilgrim does when he reaches Varanasi?

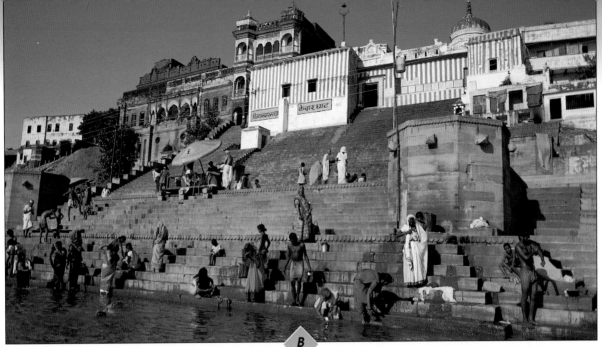

Two things, in particular, take place along the banks of the river in Varanasi. What are they?

Words to remember

Ghat   The steps or platforms at the edge of holy rivers. People bathe from the ghats which are also used in the cremation of dead bodies.

Reincarnation   The belief that the soul is reborn many times before it reaches Nirvana. This belief is shared with Sikhs and Buddhists.

Shiva   The 'kindly one'; one of the greatest Hindu gods, in murtis he is sometimes shown dancing.

Things to do

1   Picture B shows the many ghats along the bank of the River Ganges. Explain what you think a visitor to the city might expect to find taking place on these ghats as he or she walks along the river bank.

2   In your own words, write a short description of the city of Varanasi. Try to explain why it is such an important town for Hindu pilgrims.

3   Eric Newby is a traveller who has written many books. In *Slowly Down the Ganges* he writes about the holy river:

   'It is great because, to millions of Hindus it is the most sacred, venerated river on earth. To bathe in it is to wash away guilt. To drink the water, having bathed in it, and to carry away bottles of it for those who have not had the great fortune to make the pilgrimage is meritorious [praiseworthy]. To be cremated on its banks, having died there, is the wish of every Hindu. Even to ejaculate [call out] "Ganga, Ganga", at the distance of fifty-five kilometres from the river, may atone [make amends] for the sins committed during three previous lives.'

a   Two words, 'sacred' and 'venerated', are used in this extract to describe the River Ganges. Find out what they mean and write their definitions in your book.

b   What do Hindus believe happens to anyone who bathes in the waters of the River Ganges?

c   Which two things does every Hindu wish for?

d   How does a Hindu hope that he might be able to make amends for the sins of three of his previous lives?

93

Why is Amritsar important?

The Guru Granth Sahib tells all Sikhs:

'If a man goes to bathe at a place of pilgrimage with the mind of a crook and the body of a thief, his exterior will be washed by bathing, of course, but his inside will be twice as unclean. He will be like the gourd, clean on the outside but full of poison within.'

What matters, therefore, is the spiritual state in which each Sikh undertakes a pilgrimage. The journey will only draw him closer to God if he is prepared to give up his evil ways. If he does so, he may join thousands of other pilgrims travelling to the **Golden Temple** in Amritsar, confident that he will receive a blessing from God.

The Golden Temple

The city of Amritsar was founded by Guru Ram Das so that Sikhs could come to worship God. Those working on the city dug out a lake which was called 'Amrit Sarowar' (Pool of Nectar). Guru Arjan then built the Golden Temple in the middle of the lake (see picture A).

Holding a special place in the affections of all Sikhs, the Golden Temple is believed to be the 'Court of the Lord'. Gold leaf covers the outside of the building whilst inside the walls are covered with beautiful paintings. Over the gateway to the Temple is the treasury in which there used to be four sets of golden doors, jewelled canopies and umbrellas, together with the golden spades which were used to begin the desilting of the lake in 1923. All these were destroyed when the Indian Army invaded the Golden Temple complex in 1984 because of political unrest.

Invasion of the Golden Temple

Hymns from the Guru Granth Sahib are sung in the Golden Temple non-stop, day and night. The Indian Army invasion totally interrupted this. The soldiers were trying to remove Sikh militants who had been using the Temple as a fortress. Although much was lost from the treasury, the building itself suffered little damage. However, many people lost their lives in the incident.

Word to remember

Golden Temple   The centre of Sikh pilgrimage, built by the fifth Guru, Arjan, beside the Pool of Nectar.

A
Why do you think that this embroidery links the Golden Temple with these two Gurus?

Do you know

◇ what the Guru Granth Sahib has to say about the dangers of undertaking pilgrimages in the wrong frame of mind?
◇ why the location of the Golden Temple in Amritsar is spiritually so important to Sikhs?
◇ what upset Sikhs throughout the world in 1984?

What is the name given to the pool of water which surrounds the Golden Temple in Amritsar?

Things to do

1 Here are some answers to a crossword. Write down what you think the clues might have been:

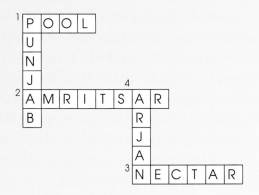

2 When asked on one occasion 'Should I go and bathe at a pilgrimage place?' Guru Nanak replied, 'God's Name is the real pilgrimage place.' Looking at the quotation from the Guru Granth Sahib at the beginning of this chapter, answer these questions:

a Why should the crook and the thief be twice as unclean after a pilgrimage as they were before going on one?

b What do you think that Guru Nanak meant when he said that 'God's Name is the real pilgrimage place'?

c If a person is prepared to give up his or her evil ways before a pilgrimage, what benefit might the holy journey have?

3 In the days of Guru Arjan, there were two main religions in India: Hinduism and Islam. Neither would allow members of the other faith to enter their holy buildings. Guru Arjan was very unhappy about this and said:

'God gives air, water and sunshine to everybody, so all have equal rights to thank God for his gifts and sing his praises. So temples should be open to all.'

a What was Guru Arjan's main reason for insisting that religious buildings should be open for everyone to worship God?

b Do you agree with Guru Arjan that temples (or any place of worship) should be open to all? Explain your answer.

Words to remember

Page references in bold indicate that the word is defined on this page in the 'Words to remember' box.